Exiles, Entrepreneurs, and Educators

SUNY series in African American Studies
―――――
John R. Howard and Robert C. Smith, editors

# Exiles, Entrepreneurs, and Educators
## African Americans in Ghana

STEVEN J. L. TAYLOR

Cover art: iStock by Getty Images

Published by State University of New York Press, Albany

© 2019 State University of New York

All rights reserved

No part of this book may be used or reproduced in any manner whatsoever without written permission. No part of this book may be stored in a retrieval system or transmitted in any form or by any means including electronic, electrostatic, magnetic tape, mechanical, photocopying, recording, or otherwise without the prior permission in writing of the publisher.

For information, contact State University of New York Press, Albany, NY
www.sunypress.edu

## Library of Congress Cataloging-in-Publication Data

Names: Taylor, Steven J. L., 1958– author.
Title: Exiles, entrepreneurs, and educators : African Americans in Ghana / Steven J. L. Taylor.
Description: Albany : State University of New York Press, 2019. | Includes bibliographical references and index.
Identifiers: LCCN 2018033274 | ISBN 9781438474717 (hardcover : alk. paper) | ISBN 9781438474700 (pbk. : alk. paper) | ISBN 9781438474724 (ebook)
Subjects: LCSH: African Americans—Ghana—History. | African Americans—Relations with Africans. | African Americans—Political activity—Ghana. | African American businesspeople—Ghana.
Classification: LCC DT510.43.A37 T39 2019 | DDC 966.700496073—dc23
LC record available at https://lccn.loc.gov/2018033274

10  9  8  7  6  5  4  3  2  1

*This book is dedicated to my grandnephews,
Melvin Charles Cross III and Maddox Tristan Cross,
who give me so much hope for the future.*

# Contents

Acknowledgments — ix

Introduction — xi

Chapter 1  African-American Migration to Africa Before 1966 — 1

Chapter 2  From Republic to Regime — 21

Chapter 3  From Regime to Republic — 35

Chapter 4  Entrepreneurs and Educators — 67

Chapter 5  Organizations Founded by African-American Expatriates — 75

Chapter 6  Summary and Outlook — 91

Notes — 103

Bibliography — 117

Index — 127

# Acknowledgments

I would like to express my sincere appreciation to those persons and institutions who assisted me throughout the research that has resulted in this book. First of all, I wish to thank the Fulbright Program of the U.S. Department of State for providing me with the financial assistance necessary to travel and spend the time in Ghana required to complete the research. I am also grateful to the School of Public Affairs of American University for granting me a sabbatical during this period of research. While in Ghana, the women and men employed at the U.S. embassy were of invaluable help to me, as were my colleagues in the Department of Political Science at the University of Ghana. I am also extremely grateful to the members of the African American Association of Ghana. Not only did many of the members of the Association consent to being interviewed, but they also provided me with friendship and support during a time when I was thousands of miles away from home.

# Introduction

### Two Stages of African-American Migration to Ghana

On March 6, 1957, Britain's African colony the Gold Coast became the independent country of Ghana, under the leadership of Prime Minister Kwame Nkrumah, who would later become President. Nkrumah had a vision of a united Africa, which would include the descendants of those who were victims of the Atlantic slave trade. Nkrumah welcomed African Americans to come to the newly independent country where they could lend their expertise and make Ghana a shining example of pan-African unity. Hundreds of African Americans heeded Nkrumah's call and took up residence in Ghana. Nearly all were staunch supporters of Nkrumah and his political party, the Convention People's Party (CPP), and some received government appointments. The African-American expatriate community was one that was very much aware of the political occurrences in their adopted country, and its members were quite concerned with the political developments in Ghana.

The situation for African-American expatriates became very precarious on February 24, 1966, when Nkrumah's government was removed from office in a military coup. The military junta rescinded Nkrumah's welcome toward Black Americans. While it was a military coup that ended Ghana's outreach toward Black Americans, it was also a military coup, occurring nearly 16 years later, which re-opened Ghana's doors to them. On the last day of 1981 a seemingly pro-Nkrumah Air Force Lieutenant, Jerry John Rawlings, seized control of Ghana's government. After Rawlings became firmly in control, he took bold measures that he hoped would improve Ghana's economy. One such measure was inviting foreigners, including African Americans, to come to Ghana to invest in its economy. Many African Americans accepted that invitation and immigrated to Ghana. Today nearly 3,000 African Americans live in or around Accra, Ghana's capital and largest city,[1] most of whom arrived subsequent to the invitation given by Flight Lieutenant (later President) Rawlings. Today's African-American community in Ghana is much larger than the community that existed during the Nkrumah days. In addition to being larger, another difference is that the new generation of expatriates is not politically active, nor is there the strong political support for Nkrumahism. This book compares the two generations of African-American expatriates, and examines why the current group is non-political, and why there is less support for the political parties that identify with the late Kwame Nkrumah.

## Relevant Literature on African-American Migration to West Africa

The topic of African Americans residing in Africa, and Ghana in particular, has been explored by a number of researchers. One of the most comprehensive works on this topic was written by James T. Campbell, and it is entitled Middle Passages: African American Journeys to Africa, 1787–2005. Campbell describes the waves of migration of Black people who left the New World to return to their ancestral continent. He looks back to the earliest days of the American Republic, when former slaves who had been emancipated by the British military were compelled to flee the United States. Many went to Canada first, and from there some departed to Sierra Leone to establish a British colony. Similarly, thousands of freed former slaves in the newly established United States went to the West African territory of Liberia, which became the first republic on the African continent. Much of my information on the earliest African-American settlers in Africa comes from *Middle Passages*.

Another wave of migration to Africa began with the independence of Ghana in 1957, which coincided with the Civil Rights Movement in the United States. In his book *American Africans in Ghana*, Kevin Gaines provides information about prominent African Americans who were dissatisfied with the slow pace of social progress in the United States, and who left the U.S. to settle in the first Sub-Saharan African nation to receive its independence in the twentieth century. Gaines looks at several exiles from the U.S. Among those are writer Richard Wright (who resided in France), civil rights attorney Pauli Murray,[2] and novelist, actor and playwright Julian Mayfield.[3] Gaines describes their efforts to negotiate the often volatile political environment in Ghana during the days of its First Republic. It is through Gaines that researchers learn of the political activities of African Americans who settled in Ghana in the 1950s and 1960s. David Levering Lewis also reports on his own experiences meeting with politically active expatriates who lived in Ghana during the Nkrumah regime. His published records of these meetings can be read in "Ghana, 1963: A Memoir," which was published in the *American Scholar*.

The 1966 ouster of Kwame Nkrumah was the start of a lengthy period of instability, marked by more coups, attempted coups, and two short-lived republics. Between 1969 and 1981 there were six different military governments, interspersed with one civilian government that lasted for only three years, and another that lasted for only two. Roger Gocking's *The History of Ghana* speaks extensively of the various military regimes of the 1960s through the 1980s, and of the two brief attempts at democratic governance. Though Gocking's work provides no coverage of the experiences of African Americans in Ghana, it does give a thorough explanation about the increasing stability that came to attract foreigners to move to Ghana. Another work that covers the various regime changes in Ghana is Volume One of Emmanuel Doe Ziorklui's *Ghana: Nkrumah to Rawlings*.

The Rawlings Era marked the beginning of the current wave of migration of African Americans to Ghana. In 2015 Justin Williams published an article in African Studies entitled "The 'Rawlings Revolution and Rediscovery of the African Diaspora in Ghana (1983–2015)." Here Williams compares the socialist pan-Africanism of Kwame Nkrumah with the neoliberal pan-Africanism of Jerry Rawlings. Williams focuses on what I include as a major theme of this book, and that is how many of those participating in the current wave of African-American migration to Ghana are involved in entrepreneurial activities, including the tourism industry. In her book *African Homecoming: Pan-African Ideology and Contested Heritage*, Katharina Schramm provides a great deal of coverage of African-American tourism to Ghana. Schramm speaks of the desire of African Americans to come to Ghana to reclaim their heritage, and how the government of Ghana has helped facilitate that reclamation by sponsoring activities such as Emancipation Day and PANAFEST. In another work, entitled "Negotiating Race: Blackness and Whiteness in the Context of Homecoming to Ghana," Schramm writes of her ethnographic study of

African-American expatriates and the degree to which they feel welcome in Ghana. In an article entitled, "Rites of Passage, Routes of Redemption: Emancipation Tourism and the Wealth of Culture," published in *Africa Today*, Jennifer Hasty also writes about Emancipation Day and how such celebrations have served to increase the number of African Americans traveling to Ghana. Hasty also writes about those African Americans who came, not as tourists, but as permanent settlers, and of the problems that some have in finding acceptance among Ghanaians.

What is missing from the existing literature about Ghana is coverage of the political proclivities of the current wave of African Americans in Ghana: those who came during the Fourth Republic, or the years leading up to the restoration of democracy. While researchers such as Kevin Gaines have written about the political activities of African Americans during the First Republic, far less is written about this topic during the Fourth Republic. Most information about African-American current participation in Ghana's politics focuses on their involvement in traditional politics, meaning the chieftaincy. George Bob-Milliar's article "Chieftaincy, Diaspora, and Development," looks at the role of the "Development Chiefs" in various villages in Akan-speaking regions in Ghana. Many of these "development chiefs" are African Americans. In the book *Relations Between Africans and African Americans: Misconceptions, Myths and Realities*, Godfrey Mwakikagile provides the most comprehensive coverage yet of the attempts of African Americans to establish a village in eastern Ghana, named Fihankra, and to install traditional leadership. In chapter 5 of this book, I provide a brief follow-up to Mwakikagile's coverage of Fihankra, and I summarize news reports about tragic events that recently occurred there, as does Mwakikagile in his latest work, entitled *The People of Ghana: Ethnic Diversity and National Unity*. I complement Mwakikagile's writings with interviews of persons closely connected with the Fihankra community.

## Ghana as a Preferred West African Destination

Though some African Americans in Ghana have settled in remote locations like Fihankra, the vast majority of those in Ghana reside in and around the capital city of Accra. There are more African Americans living in Ghana than in any other African country. Tanzania, in East Africa, is also the home to a sizable number of African Americans, but not nearly as many as in Ghana. There are several reasons why Ghana has been an attractive destination for African Americans who wish to return to the continent of their ancestors. One reason is that Ghana is on the west coast of Africa, the region of the continent where the majority of African-Americans' families originated. While very few African Americans are able to trace their direct lineage, as writer Alex Haley was able to do, there is irrefutable historical evidence that the vast majority of slaves taken to the western hemisphere came from West Africa. The southern coast of Ghana is dotted with castles that were used as a staging point for the departure of slaves headed to the New World.[4] These castles remain standing, and they are now tourist attractions. They also serve as a reminder that a large percentage of African Americans have ancestors who embarked from what is now Ghana. It is for this reason that I use the term repatriates interchangeably with the term expatriates. Conventionally those persons who leave their country of birth and settle in a different country are referred to as "expatriates." However, African Americans are moving to the land where their ancestors originated. In other words, they left their natal homeland and took up residence in their aboriginal homeland. It is for this reason that that the terms expatriate and repatriate are used interchangeably throughout this book.

The country of Senegal is also the site of a slave castle, on the country's Goree Island, but Senegal has not become a destination of African Americans seeking to settle in Africa. Hence the second reason why Ghana is a more attractive location for African-American repatriates. Ghana, formerly called the "Gold Coast," was a British colony from 1844 to 1957,[5] and English is the official language. Senegal, in contrast, is a former French colony, and the official language is French. African Americans who settle in Ghana have an easier time communicating with the local residents than they would if they settled in Senegal, Cote d'Ivoire, Togo, or other West African countries where English is not the official language. The use of English as an official language is one reason why Tanzania is also a popular location for African Americans who have repatriated to the Continent.

The third reason why Ghana has been a destination for African Americans is that Ghana was the first Sub-Saharan country to become independent during the postwar wave of decolonization, and its first head of state, Kwame Nkrumah, extended an invitation to Black Americans to settle in Ghana and assist his countrymen in building their new nation. The first generation of African-Americans to settle in Ghana began in 1957 when Nkrumah became Prime Minister (later President). One year after Ghana became independent, Nkrumah visited the U.S. and ensured African Americans of a warm welcome awaiting them in Ghana. Nkrumah spoke of "bonds of blood and kinship" that linked them to Ghana.[6] Nkrumah's invitation was taken up by writers, academicians, professionals, and political refugees. The most notable was the eminent scholar Dr. W. E. B. Du Bois, who moved to Ghana in 1961 at the age of 93. Despite his advanced age, Du Bois had suffered no decline in mental acuity, and immediately began work on an academic project entitled *Encyclopedia Africana*, a project that was funded by the Ghanaian government. Du Bois was joined by his wife, Shirley Graham Du Bois. While Dr. Du Bois was working on the encyclopedia project, Mrs. Du Bois established and directed the government-owned Ghana Broadcasting Service. Mrs. Du Bois was one of several expatriates who played prominent roles in Nkrumah's government. The Du Boises were provided a handsome residence in the upscale Cantonments section of Accra. That home is now a museum, and the compound surrounding it houses an events center, a visitors' hostel, and the headquarters of two expatriate organizations: the Diaspora Africa Forum and the African American Association of Ghana.

The positive view of the Nkrumah government was not unanimous among African-American expatriates. Nkrumah was becoming increasingly autocratic, and he was cultivating an alliance with the Soviet Union. Some African Americans were dismayed by this turn of events. One such person was the American dissident novelist Richard Wright, who had years earlier warned Nkrumah against a close alliance with the Soviet Union. Wright was a strong supporter of Nkrumah, and of pan-Africanism in general, but he nonetheless voiced his concerns in an open letter to Kwame Nkrumah.[7] When Ghana celebrated its independence in March 1957, Wright was not among those invited to attend the festivities. Another high profile African American who became disenchanted with the Nkrumah regime was Pauline "Pauli" Murray, who briefly served as a law professor at the University of Ghana. Murray left after having spent just one year in Ghana. Most Black expatriates, however, chose to remain in Ghana, and they were strong supporters of Nkrumah and his Convention People's Party government. The bulk of the approximately 300 African American expatriates who left the U.S. and migrated to Ghana did so because they saw themselves as political dissidents when they were in the U.S. In Ghana they were referred to as "the Politicals" because of their focus on political issues. The Politicals were avid supporters of the CPP.

The fate of the Politicals became precarious on February 24, 1966 when Nkrumah and his CPP government were overthrown by a U.S.-supported coup d'état carried out by the Ghanaian military and police services. The ruling junta had no sympathy toward Black American exiles. Some of the expatriates, such as Shirley Graham Du Bois, were deported, while others left before being deported. Some of those who left went to Tanzania, where they were welcomed by President Julius Nyerere, an ally of Nkrumah.

For Black Americans the situation did not improve when Ghana returned to democratic rule in 1969. The elected government of the Second Republic was run by an anti-Nkrumahist party, the Progress Party, under the leadership of Prime Minister Kofi Abrefa Busia. While establishing close ties with the rightist Nixon Administration in the U.S., and making overtures to the apartheid regime in South Africa, Busia did not reinstate Nkrumah's invitation to African Americans to help build and develop the young nation of Ghana. The welcome mat had been rolled up in 1966, and was not unfurled until the 1980s under the military regime of Air Force Lieutenant J. J. Rawlings. Rawlings had briefly been in office in 1979 after having successfully staged a coup that ousted a military regime, but he and the members of his junta returned to the barracks after an elected government was brought into office. Two years later, however, Rawlings overthrew that elected regime and returned to office, but this time there were no plans for a swift return to democracy.

## Rawlings Revives the Invitation to African Americans

The Rawlings-led military junta included junior officers such as Rawlings. It gave itself the name "Provisional National Defence Council" (PNDC), with Rawlings as Chairman and head of state. Once the PNDC became entrenched, it proposed sweeping economic and political changes. Initially Rawlings espoused leftist rhetoric that resembled that of the Nkrumah era, and he received support from many who considered themselves to be "radical Nkrumahists."[8] But less than two years after seizing power, Rawlings did an about-face and began implementing neoliberal economic policies that were pleasing to the highly industrialized creditor nations. Ghana began experiencing economic growth on the macro-level, which made it an attractive location for foreign investors. But despite the economic changes, Rawlings did not jettison the pan-Africanist philosophies, and he and his PNDC government continued their opposition to apartheid in South Africa. Moreover, the PNDC government revived Nkrumah's invitation to African Americans to settle in Ghana. The difference was that, whereas Nkrumah wanted expatriates to come help build a newly independent nation, Rawlings merely wanted them to help build up Ghana's free-market economy. He was looking for entrepreneurs, not dissidents. Many of those who heeded Rawlings's invitation came as business entrepreneurs, hence I refer to them as the "Entrepreneurials," as opposed to the "Politicals" of the Nkrumah era. Though Rawlings did not appropriate the economic policies of Nkrumah's socialist regime, he did reach out to the devotees of the first head of state, and he has tried to present himself and his followers as being in the Nkrumahist tradition. In line with Nkrumah's pan-Africanism, Rawlings went so far as to propose dual citizenship for those Black Americans wishing to reside in Ghana on a permanent basis. This would be akin to the "Law of Return" for diasporic Jews who wish to settle in Israel.

For ten years, beginning with the installation of the PNDC government, political activity was not an option for most Ghanaians. The junta did not permit the formation of political parties, nor did it allow citizens to elect a parliament. It has often been said that during this period Ghana developed a "Culture of Silence," whereby individuals refused to discuss governmental abuses out of fear of retribution.[9]

The restrictions on society were lifted in 1992 when the PNDC announced that democratic elections would be held at the end of the year, and that political parties could be formed without government intervention. The PNDC re-branded itself as the "NDC," or the "National Democratic Congress." Rawlings officially resigned his Air Force commission and ran as the NDC's presidential candidate for Ghana's Fourth Republic. The major candidates in that race were as follows: Rawlings, who was the center-left candidate; the center-right candidate, Adu Boahen, of the New Patriotic Party (NPP); and the left-of-center candidate, Hilla Limman, of the People's National Convention, an avowedly Nkrumahist political party. Limman had been the president of the Third Republic from 1979 until December 31, 1981, when he was ousted by the second Rawlings-led coup. Both the NDC and the PNC vied for the support of the Nkrumahist voters, but the NDC had the advantages that accompany incumbency.

After the votes were counted, it became apparent that Rawlings had the support of the Nkrumahists in Ghana, while Limman's PNC was a very minor party. Rawlings won the election, but his most formidable opposition came from the NPP, and that party remains the

NDC's rival for control of Ghana. The NPP follows the tradition of Nkrumah's major rival, Dr. Joseph Boakye Danquah and his successor Dr. Kofi Abrefa Busia, who was the Prime Minister of Ghana from 1969 to 1972. The NPP models itself after the Republican Party in the United States, and has adopted the elephant as its symbol, the same as the Republican Party. The NPP and the Republican Party are members of the International Democratic Union, a worldwide coalition of right-wing and center-right political parties.[10] Ghana's current NPP president, Nana Akufo-Addo, describes the NPP and the Republican Party of the United States as "sisters," and has reached out to U.S. President Donald Trump.[11] When Trump was declared the winner of the U.S. presidential election, Akufo-Addo's sent a congratulatory letter to him. This was one month prior to Ghana's presidential election, in which Akufo-Addo was hoping to unseat the incumbent, John Dramani Mahama. Akufo-Addo went on to win the 2016 election, and he became the fifth president of the Fourth Republic. Both the election and the regime change went peacefully, attesting to Ghana's stability and the strength of its democracy.

Ghana's political stability, the (P)NDC/Rawlings invitation, the country's economic growth since the 1980s, and the shared use of English

Figure 1. Steven Taylor and Nana Akufo-Addo, October 23, 2015, in Washington, DC (author's collection).

have all contributed to making Ghana an attractive destination for African Americans wishing to repatriate to the continent. There are, however, significant differences between the motives of the Nkrumah-era repatriates and those of the current era. Very few African Americans who settled in Ghana post-1981 can be referred to as "Politicals." Nkrumah encouraged African-American settlers to become involved in his government, and there were some who did. Most of those who did not take government positions were nonetheless ideologically supportive of Nkrumah and the CPP. The current group of repatriates does not include anyone who went on to become a government official. Moreover, since parliament has thus far failed to act on Rawlings's call for dual citizenship for African Americans; members of that community are not involved in formal political activities, such as voting or seeking government positions. The only voting opportunities available to repatriates is to cast absentee ballots for elections back in the United States, as I did for the 2016 state of Maryland primary elections. One purpose of this study is to determine if the current generation of repatriates was involved politically before leaving the U.S. I interviewed repatriates and asked them about their involvement back in the U.S., and if this involvement has led them to support the NDC and oppose the NPP, just as they opposed the latter's "sister party" in the United States.

Though African Americans residing in Ghana do not have the opportunity to vote, Ghana today is a democratic country by any international standard, hence persons residing there have the opportunity to participate in non-voting political activities. Wong, Ramakrishnan, Lee, and Junn identify four non-conventional means of political participation, means that are available in a democratic environment, such as in the United States and in Ghana. The four means are (1) political donations, (2) contacting government officials, (3) community activism, and (4) protest.[12] To those four, I add editorializing, broadcasting, and blogging. These are opportunities afforded to both citizens and non-citizens alike. In this study I conducted interviews with African-American repatriates in Ghana to determine how extensively they are involved in political participation, even if it is one or more of the non-conventional means of political involvement. I asked my respondents if they have availed themselves of these democratic opportunities in Ghana, and if so how have they leaned politically. They were also asked if their allegiance to the Democratic Party in the U.S. translated to an allegiance to Ghana's center-left party, the National Democratic Congress. My hypothesis was that that those African Americans who are politically active (albeit unofficially), and those who are inactive but who have political leanings, would affiliate with the NDC. The NDC is an offshoot of Kwame Nkrumah's CPP, and it was Nkrumah's regime that extended the invitation to African Americans to settle in Ghana, an invitation renewed by NDC founder Jerry Rawlings. This is what led me to hypothesize that politically active African Americans in Ghana would be supportive of the NDC, just as that first generation of repatriates affiliated itself with the CPP.

## Methodology of the Study

The methodology used for this study was ethnographic research conducted through participant observation and through interviews. I spent the winter and spring of 2016 in Ghana on a fellowship provided by the Fulbright program of the United States Department of State. Two years prior to my extended stay in Ghana, I visited the country. This trip was conducted in May 2014, and during that visit I attended three gatherings of the African American Association of Ghana (AAAG), an organization founded in 1981. The AAAG is an organization of expatriates from the United States and assists them as they settle in Ghana. The Association sponsors cultural, social, and religious events, sometimes in conjunction with the U.S. embassy. Though I had been to Ghana seven times prior to 2014, I had not involved myself with the AAAG.

I returned to Ghana at 8:00 a.m. on January 17, 2017. That afternoon I attended AAAG's monthly meeting, and I joined the organization. I immediately became active with an AAAG committee that was planning events for the upcoming Black History Month. Throughout the four months that I was in Ghana, I was very active with the AAAG, and I interviewed many of its members. Those interviews provided me with much of the information for this study. Not all the respondents were AAAG members, but the members of the Association provided me with the bulk of the information about twenty-first-century life for African-American repatriates in Ghana. There were 34 respondents, of whom 21 were females and 13 were males. Half of the female respondents were spouses of Ghanaians, while only two of the male respondents fell into that category. Two of the respondents (both females) were not from the U.S., but were of Caribbean origin and were affiliated with the Ghana Caribbean Association (GCA), an organization similar to AAAG but which works with expatriates of Caribbean origin. I also utilized two news articles in which the subjects were African-American females living in Ghana. Readers will observe that when respondents are quoted, I am careful to avoid including information that will identify who they are. For that reason their gender is very rarely disclosed; rather, they are referred to as "the respondent" or "the interviewee." This is in line with an agreement that I made to preserve their anonymity.

Ten of the 21 females left the U.S. with their Ghana-born spouses, while only one of the males fell into that category. All but one of the respondents came with the second wave of African Americans moving to Ghana, while the other came in the mid-1960s, during the regime of Kwame Nkrumah. Those respondents who were members of the Ghana Caribbean Association provided me with a perspective of repatriates from the Islands of the Caribbean.

In Ghana I encountered a small number of African Americans who are affiliated with the All African People's Revolutionary Party (AAPRP). The AAPRP is a pan-Africanist socialist organization that adheres to the philosophies of Kwame Nkrumah. The organization has chapters in the U.S., Ghana, and several other countries. I refer to the AAPRP expatriates living in Ghana today as modern "Politicals." While they are only a small number among the expatriates, their presence in Ghana demonstrates that the current cohort of African Americans in Ghana is a politically diverse group. Among the expatriates' numbers are Politicals, Entrepreneurials, and spouses of Ghanaians, with these groups overlapping one another.

During the interviews, the respondents were asked about their political involvement back in the United States, including voting, protest, contacting officials, or campaign contributions. I also asked them about their partisan affiliation in the U.S., whether they were affiliated with the Democratic Party, the Republican Party, or if they had no affiliation with either of those two major U.S. parties. I would then ask them about their involvement in Ghanaian politics, where their involvement would exclude voting. Though they did not vote in Ghana, I asked them about their partisan preferences, whether they supported the National Democratic Congress, the New Patriotic Party, or one of the smaller parties. Many of the respondents were not involved in any political activities, but they did express a preference toward one of the political parties. There are three reasons why I hypothesized that American repatriates would lean toward the NDC. The first reason is that the NDC claims the Nkrumahist mantle, and the president at that time, John Mahama, came from a staunchly Nkrumahist family. His father, Emmanuel Mahama, had been a CPP parliamentarian during the First Republic, and during the Third Republic he was an adviser to President Hilla Limman, a Nkrumahist.[13] Since it was Nkrumah who originated the invitation to African Americans to migrate to Ghana, my assumption was that many of the repatriates would have a preference for the NDC, which can be deemed as a Nkrumahist party. A second reason why I hypothesize that African Americans favor the NDC is because it was the party's founder, Jerry Rawlings, who reinstated the Nkrumah-era invitation to Black Americans to come to Ghana. A final basis for my hypothesis is that the NDC occupies a similar position on the Ghanaian ideological continuum that the Democratic Party occupies on the U.S. continuum. Both the NDC and the Democratic Party are center-left parties, while their respective opponents, the NPP and the Republican Parties are rightist parties. The Democratic Party commands the loyalty of close to 90 percent of African Americans in U.S. presidential elections. Black Americans' near-unanimous loyalty to the Democratic Party reaches down to the local level. Black voters in the U.S. shun the Republican Party, even when that party sponsors Black candidates for election. An example at the local level is Gary, Indiana, a city where the population was 80 percent African American. In 1995 a white attorney, Scott King, won the Democratic nomination for mayor. He was opposed by a Black Democrat, Marion Williams, who ran as an independent. King overwhelmingly defeated Williams, receiving over 77 percent of the vote, to only 18 percent for Williams.[14] On the statewide level, in 1986 a popular Black Democrat, Wayne County Executive William Lucas, switched parties and received the Republican nomination for Governor. Lucas had longstanding ties to Michigan's African Americans, having served as Sheriff and later County Executive of predominantly Black Wayne County (which includes Detroit). He was consistently supported by African-American voters until he changed parties. Black voters in Michigan voted for his White Democratic Party opponent, James Blanchard, who won the race.[15]

The current and previous Republican U.S. presidents (Donald Trump and George W. Bush, respectively) were very unpopular among African Americans, but they received strong support from the current and previous NPP presidents (Nana Akufo-Addo and John Kufuor). As previously stated, when Trump was declared the winner of the 2016 U.S. presidential election, Akufo-Addo sent him a very laudatory letter, congratulating him on his victory and expressing his joy that the

Republican Party simultaneously maintained its grip on the United States Congress. The previous NPP president, John A. Kufuor, also showed his affinity toward the Republican Party by designating a major highway as the "George W. Bush Highway," after the previous Republican president of the United States.[16] Prior to conducting this study, my belief was that African Americans in Ghana would reject the NPP just as African Americans in the U.S. have rejected its "sister party." Therefore, the working hypothesis was that African Americans in Ghana, whether they are politically involved or not, have a preference for the National Democratic Congress, and that those who are involved in political activities do so on behalf of the NDC.

# 1

# African-American Migration to Africa Before 1966

## Migrations to Sierra Leone and Liberia

For more than a century before Nkrumah's invitation to Black Americans, there had been waves of African Americans repatriating to West Africa. Perhaps the best known was the founding of the U.S. colony of Liberia, which became independent in 1846. Even earlier than the establishment of Liberia, there were African Americans who had helped set up a British Colony in Sierra Leone, to the immediate east of what would later become Liberia. Some of the repatriates who had helped found Sierra Leone had lived in slavery in Great Britain's southern colonies of North America. These colonies would later become the southern states of an independent United States. During the Revolutionary War that the United States waged against Great Britain, the British offered emancipation to those slaves who would take up arms and fight under the Union Jack as subjects of the Crown. There were many slaves who did so, thus receiving their manumission from forced servitude. Their position became quite precarious when the war ended in favor of the United States. Knowing that these Black soldiers of the Crown could not remain in the U.S., the British government initially offered them land in in the Canadian province of Nova Scotia. They left their homes in the Carolinas and elsewhere and migrated to Nova Scotia, establishing a community centered in the city of Birchtown.[1] A smaller number of the former slaves crossed the Atlantic and settled in Great Britain, where they lived hardscrabble lives of poverty and deprivation.[2]

The climate and soil of Nova Scotia proved to be inhospitable for persons who were accustomed to farming and cultivating crops in a sub-tropical region of the continent. The British government therefore decided to allow them to repatriate to West Africa and help the Crown establish a colony there. That colony was Sierra Leone, an area that had been earlier visited by Portuguese explorers.[3] In Sierra Leone the repatriates were able to return to their former agricultural pursuits that they had left behind in the U.S. South. They also brought their Christian religion and their language, a variant of English, but with West African words and terms interspersed. That language, commonly known as "Gullah," is quite similar to the "Krio" spoken today by Sierra Leonean descendants of repatriates from North America.[4]

Meanwhile in the United States, many whites were concerned about the presence of emancipated former slaves. Following the British example, certain government officials, philanthropists, and religious figures, both Black and White, chose to establish a U.S. colony on the west coast of Africa. Under the auspices of the American Colonization Society (ACS), more than 20,000 African Americans were sent to Liberia between the years of 1821 and 1910.[5] In 1847 Liberia became independent of the U.S., making it the first Sub-Saharan African country to gain its independence from a Western power. For the next six decades it remained a destination for African Americans sent by the American Colonization Society.

After the American Colonization Society folded in 1910, it would be almost fifty years before there would be another significant exodus of African Americans to West Africa. The ACS-controlled exodus was one that was led by forces external to the Black community, and could not be deemed to have been voluntary. For some the choice was to leave for Liberia or remained enslaved in the U.S. For others, remaining in the U.S. meant subjection to constant persecution and denial of the means to survive. As was the case with Jews who fled Czarist-inspired pogroms, African Americans were victims of "push factors" that forced them to emigrate from their homeland.

## Ghana Replaces Liberia

The next migratory wave of African Americans to their ancestral continent began in the late-1950s when Ghana became the first Sub-Saharan African nation to receive independence from a European power. Prime

Minister Nkrumah was a pan-Africanist who believed in the linked fate of people of African descent, including those residing in the western hemisphere. Due to his ten years of living in the U.S., Nkrumah had developed an affinity toward Black Americans, whom he had lived among and from whom he had received his collegiate education. After becoming established as the leader of an independent Ghana, Nkrumah extended an invitation to African Americans to migrate to Ghana and help him build and develop this neophyte among the international community of nations. Thus began that wave of migration of African Americans to West Africa. While push factors precipitated the previous departure of Black Americans, this wave was lured by the "pull factors" of an enthusiastic pan-African head of state.

Nkrumah could relate well to Diasporan Africans because he had spent his early adulthood away from the continent of Africa. He received his higher education in the United States and had deep personal ties with African Americans. He acquired his undergraduate education at Lincoln University in Pennsylvania, which claims to be the oldest historically Black college/university (HBCU) in the U.S. (a claim it shares with Wilberforce University in Ohio).[6] While at Lincoln, Nkrumah became involved in the social life of the student body, and was a member of Phi Beta Sigma, an African-American social fraternity that was founded at Howard University in 1914.[7] Nkrumah spent ten years in the United States (1935–1945), during which time he received two baccalaureate degrees from Lincoln University and two master's degrees from the University of Pennsylvania.[8] He also worked as an itinerant Presbyterian minister and as a professor at Lincoln University.[9] Nkrumah's second degree from Lincoln, a Bachelor of Sacred Theology, was from the school's seminary. Such a degree required three years of study beyond a baccalaureate in another field, similar to the law school paradigm. While teaching at Lincoln, Nkrumah was simultaneously a PhD student in philosophy at the University of Pennsylvania. At Lincoln he was a highly regarded professor, and he was awarded the distinction of "The Most Outstanding Professor of the Year."[10] Things did not go as well for him at the University of Pennsylvania. He had begun a dissertation entitled *Mind and Thought in Primitive Society: A Study in Ethno-philosophy, with Special References to the Akan Peoples of the Gold Coast, West Africa*. While in the midst of writing the dissertation, it was rejected by the faculty in his academic department.[11] Rather than begin a second dissertation, Nkrumah left the University of Pennsylvania, and in May 1945 he departed the U.S. on a ship headed to London.

Nkrumah enrolled as a graduate student in the London School of Economics, with the intention of studying Law and receiving a PhD in philosophy.[12] He abandoned both of those academic goals as he became involved in political activities. In London he immersed himself in the activities of organizations that promoted the concerns of Africans. He became Vice President of the West African Students Union (WASU), and he became a secretary of the "Organization Committee" that was planning a Pan-African Congress to take place in October 1945. Through the Congress, Nkrumah befriended African-American activist and scholar W. E. B. Du Bois, who served as the chair. After the Congress concluded, Nkrumah became General Secretary of the West African National Congress.[13] Nkrumah shared the main objective of these organizations, which was independence for his native Gold Coast and the remainder of the continent of Africa. Nkrumah's political activities aroused the attention of African pro-independence advocates. In 1947 he was asked to return to the Gold Coast to accept the job of General Secretary of the United Gold Coast Convention (UGCC), an organization that was committed to nonviolent action in the struggle for independence from Great Britain. Nkrumah accepted that offer and returned to the Gold Coast after having been abroad for twelve years.

Nkrumah remained with the UGCC for nearly two years, but he had differences with the other leaders of the organization. On June 12, 1949, he officially split from the UGCC and announced the launching of another party, the Convention People's Party.[14] The CPP immediately became the principal rival of the UGCC. This was a struggle between the conservative intelligentsia and the chiefs (the UGCC) versus impatient youths and radical idealists (the CPP). The difference between the two parties was exemplified by their conflicting slogans. The UGCC's slogan was "Self-government within the shortest possible time," while the CPP's slogan was "Full self-government now!"[15]

Though not yet willing to grant independence to its mineral rich colony, the British did allow elections in the Gold Coast, the first taking place in 1951. The CPP contested the election, under the leadership of Kwame Nkrumah, while the UGCC was led by Dr. Joseph Boakye Danquah, an erstwhile ally of Nkrumah. The British developed a constitution for the Gold Coast, providing for an 84-member legislature, wherein only 38 would be elected, and the other 46 appointed by the colonial government. Of those 38 contested seats, the CPP won 34. Kwame Nkrumah, who was at the time imprisoned for nonviolent actions against the colonial government, was released and asked to join the government as the Prime Minister.[16] The 1951 election was the first of three preceding independence in 1957. In the next election, held in 1954, the longstanding ethnic divisions were reflected in the partisan allegiances. The CPP was the only party that had a following throughout the different regions of Ghana, whereas all of the other parties were regionally based. The largest of the opposition parties was the National Liberation Movement (NLM), which was led by Dr. Kofi Abrefa Busia. The NLM was a political party that was based among the Ashanti ethnic group (also called the Asante), and was supported by the followers of J. B. Danquah. Of the 104 seats contested in 1954, 79 went to the CPP. The last election prior to independence was held in July 1956. The CPP continued its streak by winning 71 of the 104 seats.[17]

On March 6, 1957, the British formally surrendered control, and the colony of the Gold Coast became the independent nation of Ghana. Prime Minister Kwame Nkrumah was now the head of government, but Ghana remained a part of the British Commonwealth, and the British monarch continued on as the head of state. Queen Elizabeth II was a mere figurehead, just as she was in the British Isles and in the independent dominions such as Canada and Australia. As the titular head of state, she attended Ghana's independence ceremonies and took part in the pomp and pageantry. The ceremony was attended by dignitaries and celebrities from throughout the world, including some prominent African Americans. Among those African Americans in attendance were civil rights leader Dr. Martin Luther King, trade union and civil rights leader A. Philip Randolph (a fraternity brother of Nkrumah), Claude Barnett, who headed the Associated Negro Press, U.S. Congressman Adam Clayton Powell, U.N. Undersecretary Ralph Bunche, Ebony magazine publisher John Johnson, and Lincoln University President Horace Mann Bond. Bond was the father of Julian Bond, who would become an icon in the Civil Rights Movement. Scholar and activist W. E. B. Du Bois was also invited, but the U.S. government denied him a passport to travel abroad.[18] Not invited was Richard Wright. While supportive of the cause of pan-Africanism and of Ghana's independence, Wright did not withhold his frank critiques and suggestions for advancement of the newly independent nation. His candor cost him an invitation to this momentous event.[19]

The invitation of noted African Americans was a foreshadowing of Nkrumah's outreach to that community and of his invitation to them to repatriate to Ghana to help build and develop his embryonic state. For pan-Africanists living in the United States, Ghana was the natural choice of a country for repatriation to Africa. It was the place from which many of their ancestors departed from the Mother Land, English was the official language, and the head of state extended his welcome to them. Hundreds of African Americans fled the U.S. and sought refuge in Nkrumah's Ghana.

In many ways, Kwame Nkrumah was a voluntary protégé of W. E. B. Du Bois, who was the most preeminent African-American scholar during Nkrumah's lifetime. It was Du Bois who adjured privileged and educated African Americans to assume responsibility for the leadership and uplifting of the race. Du Bois called this advantaged group the "Talented Tenth," and he gave them this charge:

> The Talented Tenth of the Negro race must be made leaders of thought and missionaries of culture among their people. . . . The Negro race, like all other races, is going to be saved by its exceptional men.[20]

Nkrumah appealed to this "exceptional" group of Black Americans to return to their ancestral homeland and help build the newly independent nation that he was leading. Though Nkrumah described himself as a Marxian socialist, he did not appeal to the ordinary masses to come to Ghana. This wave of repatriation would be unlike those that brought Black people to Sierra Leone and Liberia. Nkrumah was not looking for farmers and laborers, but for professors, engineers, physicians, writers, and architects. Though Nkrumah was sensitive to the plight of the Black American masses (having lived in the U.S. where he faced the indignities of segregation, which is nicknamed "Jim Crow"), the reality was that Ghana was a developing country that was emerging from colonial rule. Ghana was not in an economic position to accommodate a large number of refugees. However, due to the rampant McCarthyism in the U.S., there were academicians and others from the proverbial "Talented Tenth" who were facing persecution in the U.S., and who were ripe for repatriation to a country whose leader shared their political ideology. For these members of the intelligentsia, the push factor spurring their emigration from the U.S. was racial discrimination and political repression, while the pull factor was a sense of pride in their ancestral homeland.[21]

The most well-known member of Ghana's Black American intelligentsia was Dr. Du Bois himself. Du Bois finally had his U.S. passport reinstated, and in the summer of 1960, the 92-year-old intellectual made his first trip to Ghana, accompanied by his wife, Shirley Graham Du Bois. The Du Boises were there to watch Prime Minister Nkrumah become President Nkrumah. In a plebiscite held earlier that year, the voters of Ghana had adopted a new constitution and become a republic, ending the last official vestiges of their colonial ties to Great Britain. The new constitution eliminated the post of prime minister and replaced it with that of president, who would serve as both head of state and head of government. Moreover, the position was more powerful than that of prime minister. Nkrumah ran for president against J. B. Danquah, whose "United Party" was a compilation of the former National Liberation Movement (based in the Ashanti Region) and other ethnic-based parties. Nkrumah won the election, and on July 1, 1960, he was inaugurated as president under the First Republic. The Du Boises attended the festivities. Fifteen months later, on October 1, 1961, the couple left the U.S. permanently and returned to Ghana to live. On the day of their departure, Dr. Du Bois became a member of the Communist Party USA, joining his wife, who was already a member. The two then departed for Accra, where Dr. Du Bois would spend the remaining two years of his life.[22]

Du Bois was one of several African-American immigrants who had achieved some level of fame back in the United States. In 1905 he headed the Niagara Movement, which led to the establishment of the National Association for the Advancement of Colored People (NAACP).[23] Du Bois was also a noted sociologist and well-respected scholar. In 1895 he received his PhD in sociology from Harvard University, the first African American to receive a PhD from that university. He went on to distinguish himself as an academician, and he developed a political outlook that was both socialist and pan-Africanist.

## African Americans Answer Nkrumah's Call

Du Bois's left-wing political stance was not uncommon among African-American expatriates, nor was it in any way unwelcome by Nkrumah and his followers. In his autobiography, Nkrumah proclaimed that he was both a "Marxist" and a "Christian."[24] His invitation to Black Americans attracted many leftists who were vocal about their ideology. Those in this wave of repatriates to Ghana came to be known as "the Politicals." Some, such as Du Bois, had fled the U.S. due to Cold War persecution of those known to have or thought to have communist sympathies. The year of 1961, when the Du Boises repatriated to Ghana, was the year when other "Politicals" arrived in Ghana. Author and poet Maya Angelou, an expatriate who was then living in Ghana, dubbed them as "Revolutionist Returnees."[25] Some of them had once been members of the NAACP, but had been purged from the civil rights organization because of their left-wing political philosophies. Du Bois fell into that category. Though he played a crucial role in the founding of the NAACP, he was later expelled from the organization. He later became deeply involved in the Council on African Affairs, serving as its vice president. His work with the Council led to him being prosecuted by the U.S. government. In 1946–47 the Council participated in a canned food drive to help South Africans during a famine in that country. Because the Council worked with the African National Congress in this famine relief effort, it was accused of violating the Foreign Agents Registration Act. The council was ordered to turn over its list of donors, but they disbanded rather than comply with that directive. This led to the prosecution of Du Bois and Dr. Alphaeus Hunton, the Council's Executive Secretary. In 1961 Hunton left the U.S. and joined Du Bois in Ghana.[26]

Despite his advanced age, Dr. Du Bois did not repatriate to Ghana to enjoy a leisurely retirement. He moved there to launch the *Encyclopedia Africana,* a project conceptualized by Nkrumah. The President created a government office with the task of creating this encyclopedia, which would be a comprehensive work about Africans and their continent. Nkrumah asked Du Bois to head up this task.[27] The Du Boises were provided a home in Accra.[28] On February 23, 1963, fourteen months after leaving the United States, Du Bois became a Ghanaian citizen. On that same day, which was also his 95th birthday, he was awarded an honorary doctorate from the University of Ghana.[29] Six months later, on August 27, 1963, Dr. Du Bois passed away.[30]

Du Bois and many of the other exiles from the U.S. had settled into various professional occupations, but they continued to place a priority on politics. This is why they were dubbed the "Politicals." James T. Campbell referred to Du Bois as "the doyen of the Politicals."[31] Leslie Lacy describes the "Politicals" thusly:

> All were religiously loyal to Nkrumah, zealously rationalizing his political moves, and generally, if not always ostensibly, following the ruling party's line. . . . [T]hey had a direct line to the President, as well as intimate associations with some of his key advisors. The President used their skills, including their literary talents for speech writing; took their advice rather seriously. In every sense, they identified with and were a part of the Ghanaian ruling elite.[32]

The Politicals also brought with them some of the practical skills needed in a developing country. There were Drs. Robert and Sara Lee, both of whom were dentists. They had gone to Lincoln University and the University of Pennsylvania with Kwame Nkrumah. When their friend became Ghana's head of state, the Lees moved their dental practice from New York City to Accra.[33] One notable physician who came to Ghana was a Puerto Rican woman named Ana Livia Cordero, who accompanied her husband Julian Mayfield, a writer and actor who was regarded as a leader among the expatriates.[34] Dr. Cordero took a government position with the Ministry of Health.[35] There was a plumbing contractor by the name of Lou Gardner, who worked with electrical contractors Carlos Allston and Frank Robertson.[36] Maya Angelou describes Robertson as having a "fierce devotion to Nkrumah,"[37] which was the case with most of the American repatriates of that era. Two other expatriates who helped establish Ghana's construction industry were architects Jerry Bard and Max Bond, with the latter working directly under Nkrumah.[38] Bond was the cousin of Julian Bond and the nephew of Lincoln University President Horace Mann Bond. There were also farmers who moved into the countryside, away from the capital city of Accra.[39] The vocation most highly represented among the expatriates was the teaching profession. The new government pledged to provide free public education, and teachers came to help the CPP fulfill that pledge.[40] A number of the repatriates became employed as professors at the University of Ghana. There were historians David Levering Lewis and Nell Irvin Painter. Joining them at the University were philosopher Preston King, political scientist Martin Kilson, art historian Sylvia Boone, and anthropologist St. Clair Drake. All of these professors went on to develop distinguished careers as academicians.[41] Other professors employed at the University of Ghana were Wendell Jean Pierre, a professor of French, and Leslie Lacy, who taught

Political Science. Maya Make (later to become Maya Angelou) worked as an office assistant at the University's Institute for African Studies.[42]

A typical expatriate story was that of Preston King of Albany, Georgia, who had fled the U.S. to escape conscription into the military. In the 1950s King was working on his doctorate from the London School of Economics. While in London, the Dougherty County, Georgia, draft board ordered him to report for induction into the U.S. armed forces. Having been in school, King had previously been granted an exemption from conscription, and he applied for an extension, and was initially granted one. The draft board in Dougherty County rescinded that extension when they discovered that King was Black.[43] Not only was he denied the exemption, but in their correspondence with him the members of the draft board refused to address him as "Mister." King did not report for induction; hence, the U.S. government revoked his passport, while the British government did likewise with his visa. The Ghanaian government provided him with a passport, so he fled to that country and joined the faculty at the University of Ghana.[44] Another draft resister was Bill Sutherland, a pacifist who had been sentenced to four years in prison for refusing induction into the armed forces. His sentence was twice the sentence meted out to White draft resisters, and he served three years before being released from prison. He went to Ghana in 1956 and served as Chief of Staff for Komla A. Gbedmah, who concurrently served as Nkrumah's Finance Minister and a member of the national legislature.[45] The ranks of the repatriates also included two deserters from the armed forces. Ray Kea left the military after witnessing physical brutality against Black soldiers who dated European women while stationed in Europe. Another deserter was Ray Levering Lewis who left his military post in Germany and fled to Ghana.[46]

Julian Mayfield, the unofficial head of the African-American expatriates, was also a refugee from the U.S. government. In 1961 Mayfield was charged with assisting in the kidnapping of a White couple in Monroe, North Carolina. The person Mayfield was accused of assisting was Robert Williams, who had provided shelter to the White couple as they were pursued by angry Black residents during a night of intense racial volatility in Monroe. When the situation calmed down, the couple was able to leave Williams's home, but Williams was charged with kidnapping the couple, and Mayfield was listed as an accomplice. Both Williams and Mayfield fled to Canada; from there Williams left for asylum in Cuba.[47] Mayfield received asylum in Ghana. In Ghana he utilized his writing skills and became editor of the *African Review*, Ghana's leading magazine.[48] He also became a very close advisor to Nkrumah.[49] The French editor for that magazine was Julia Wright Herve, the daughter of Richard Wright.[50]

While some repatriates were fleeing imminent prosecution, others voluntarily left the U.S. to escape political persecution. This period corresponded with the Cold War in the United States, when anti-leftist repression was at its peak. Kevin Gaines describes Ghana as a "magnet" for African Americans who were frustrated by the restrictions that the Cold War had placed upon them.[51] Dr. Du Bois was the most prominent of the refugees from the Cold War, but there were others, such as trade unionist Vicki Garvin[52] and Dr. William Alphaeus Hunton, who left a position as an English professor at Howard University, and moved to Ghana, where he became Executive Secretary of the left-leaning Council on Economic Affairs.[53] Tom Feelings was a caricature artist whose cartoons offered a brutal critique of "bourgeois" Ghanaians who opposed Nkrumah.[54] The repatriates tended to be left-leaning in their politics, and their ranks included communists, socialists, pacifists, pan-Africanists, color-blind liberals, and Black Power advocates.[55]

There were other repatriates with talents in the arts and humanities, and, like Mayfield, their skills were utilized by Nkrumah's government. Leslie Lacy said that "The President used their skills, including their literary talents, for speech writing; took their advice seriously. In every sense, they identified with and were a part of the Ghanaian ruling elite."[56] Shirley Graham Du Bois was the founding director of Ghana Television (GTV).[57] In late-1963 she invited novelist William Gardner Smith to come from the U.S. to help start GTV.[58] He and his family arrived in Ghana in September of 1964.[59] Smith was very impressed by the prominence of the African-American community in Ghana. While there were only 120 African Americans in Ghana at that time, Smith found them to be in very high positions in the country. They were highly trained and talented individuals who served as artists, writers, scholars, technologists, and electronics specialists. Smith stated that there were "mostly pretty well-trained people, numbering maybe thirty,"[60] which would have been 25 percent of the African-American contingent in Ghana. Smith became "Assistant Editor-in-Chief" of GTV, and in less than a year he was given the position of "Director of the Institute of Journalism."[61]

As exiles invited by Kwame Nkrumah, most of the African Americans in Ghana were supportive of the Convention People's Party and of Nkrumah. James Campbell writes that, "Almost by definition, those who came to Ghana supported Nkrumah, at least initially."⁶² Some later became disillusioned with Nkrumah's increasing autocratic tendencies, but most of the African Americans held Nkrumah in very high esteem. David Jenkins writes that, "Nkrumah came to find that he received more loyalty from [Black Americans] than from many senior Ghanaian figures. They shared his vision of a united Africa."⁶³ Leslie Lacy is not as kind when describing the Politicals' devotion to Nkrumah. Lacy referred to them as "professional protesters" who were zealous adherents of the CPP, and who defended Nkrumah's actions, even when such actions came under criticism from many others in Ghana and elsewhere.⁶⁴

Though the Politicals appeared united in their support of the president of Ghana, they were not nearly as enthusiastic about the president of the U.S. Many Black American leaders living in the U.S. viewed President John F. Kennedy as an ally in their fight for equal opportunity, and they were careful not to criticize him during their historic "March on Washington," held on August 28, 1963. At the very same time, Black Americans in Ghana held a sympathy demonstration that targeted the U.S. embassy. Their demonstration, led by Julian Mayfield, condemned the Kennedy Administration's policies in Cuba and Vietnam, its appeasement of the racist apartheid regime in South Africa, and the Administration's failure to move forward on civil rights legislation.⁶⁵ The demonstrators went so far as to jeer the soldiers who raised the U.S. flag. They also presented a written protest to the secretary of the United States' ambassador to Ghana.⁶⁶ Campbell believes that the sympathy march may have been the largest single gathering of expatriates.⁶⁷ This controversial demonstration was preceded by an earlier protest in which a group of Black Americans boycotted the U.S. embassy's Independence Day celebration due to the fact that Black Americans had not yet received their independence.⁶⁸ W. E. B. Du Bois was not present at the sympathy march; he had died one day earlier at the age of 95. His death was announced during the March on Washington.

During the following year, some of the Politicals formed an organization called the "Malcolm X Committee," chaired by Julian Mayfield and vice-chaired by Maya Make. This committee was formed in anticipation of a visit to Ghana by Malcolm X. When Malcolm arrived in Ghana, he visited Mayfield's home where he met with other repatriates from the U.S. The repatriates later introduced him to cabinet members of the Ghanaian government. Malcolm X also visited the homes of prominent repatriates Lesley Lacy, Drs. Sarah and Bobby Lee, and Alphaeus and

Dorothy Hunton. The recently widowed Shirley Graham Du Bois was able to arrange a visit between Malcolm X and Kwame Nkrumah.[69] Malcolm X, who had recently split from the Nation of Islam, was in the process of building a nonsectarian organization, the Organization of Afro-American Unity (OAAU), and while in Ghana he formed a chapter among the repatriates.[70] The OAAU was an example of Nkrumahism in North America. Malcolm X's vision was for the OAAU to have a seat on the Organization of African Unity (OAU), which was Nkrumah's brainchild in his efforts to forge a united Africa. The OAU included representatives from the different nations in Africa. Malcolm X's goal was for the OAAU to serve as the OAU's representative of persons of African descent who lived in the western hemisphere. The name given to the organization, "*Afro-American* Unity," also reflects Malcolm X's support for Nkrumah, for it was Nkrumah who coined the term "Afro-Americans" to describe U.S.-born persons of African descent.[71]

The Politicals tended to be pan-African in outlook, and they voiced their support for liberation movements throughout Africa. This was first demonstrated in 1960 when Western-backed military forces overthrew the government of the Congo and assassinated Prime Minister Patrice Lumumba. The Politicals sided with the Nkrumah government in supporting the regime of the fallen Prime Minister.[72] Similarly, when the White minority government of Rhodesia unilaterally declared its independence from Britain, some of the Politicals heeded Nkrumah's call for the mobilization of a People's Army, even though this put them at risk of losing their U.S. citizenship.[73] They also developed a close political and social relationship with refugees and freedom fighters from apartheid South Africa.[74] Lacy states that Julian Mayfield was the "unofficial leader of this contingent" of African Americans and South African freedom fighters.[75] His involvement in demonstrations, along with his columns criticizing U.S. policy and supporting social development, led the staff of the U.S. embassy to view Mayfield as the most reprehensible member of the African-American expatriate community in Ghana.[76]

## The Erosion of Democracy

Due to their steadfast loyalty to Kwame Nkrumah, many (though not all) African-American repatriates overlooked the increasing authoritarianism of the Ghanaian president. Ghana was devolving into a dictatorship, with

Nkrumah amassing more power for himself. From the time Nkrumah split from the UGCC, he faced opposition, which he saw as a threat to his hold on power. What prevented the opposition from defeating Nkrumah at the polls was that his political adversaries were divided along ethnic lines. The largest opposing party was the National Liberation Movement, but the NLM's support was primarily confined to members of the Ashanti tribe. The other opposition parties were also ethnic-based. This tribalization of political parties has plagued postcolonial Africa. Africa's state boundaries were externally imposed by European negotiators at the Conference of Berlin, which took place in 1884–85. During this Conference the major European powers created the boundaries between their colonies. These boundaries paid little attention to ethnic, religious, and cultural divisions. The residents of Africa were ignored while European negotiators sat in Germany's capital and carved up Africa primarily for the convenience of the soon-to-be occupying nations. People who identified themselves by their ethnicity were now forced to accept colonial boundaries that forced them to live under one central government whose domain included groups that had never identified with each other, and who were at times at enmity with one another. When the colonial powers withdrew in the 1950s and 1960s, they granted these colonies independence on the basis of boundaries they had arbitrarily imposed seventy-five to eighty years earlier. This was forced multi-ethnicity that made national unity difficult when the colonies became independent states. Political parties masked ethnic divisions, and elections became low-intensity inter-ethnic conflicts.

Ghana has not witnessed the ethnic violence seen in other African nations, but ethnicity has shaped its political cleavage structure. During the 1950s, in the years leading up to independence, the only major party that attracted supporters from all regions of Ghana was the ruling party, the Convention People's Party. The CPP had a commanding majority in parliament, which allowed Nkrumah to have his legislative agenda passed without delays or impediments. The major opposition party, the National Liberation Movement, drew most of its support from the Ashanti Region. The Northern People's Party was concentrated in the northern regions of Ghana; the Muslim Action Party was allied with the Northern People's Party, and it drew its support from Muslims throughout Ghana.[77] The Anlo Youth Organization and the Togoland Congress were based in the Volta Region, among members of the Ewe ethnic group. In Accra, the homeland of the Ga people, was the Ga Shifimo Kpee Party. These groups were in opposition to the CPP, but they were not united in their opposition. In December 1957, in a bid to put an end to his opposition, Nkrumah secured passage of the "Avoidance of Discrimination Act," which outlawed all parties that received their primary support from within one ethnic or religious group.[78] While Nkrumah may have intended to use the law to eliminate the opposition parties, the effect of the law was to strengthen them. The opposition parties united to form the United Party (UP), under the leadership of J. B. Danquah.[79]

Seven months after passing the Avoidance of Discrimination Act, Nkrumah's parliament passed the "Preventive Detention Act" (PDA). Under the PDA, persons could be arrested and detained without trial, and kept in detention for up to five years for conduct deemed to be detrimental to the security of Ghana.[80] The Nkrumah regime used this law to detain prominent members of the United Party. In 1959 Nkrumah proclaimed that "The Convention People's Party is Ghana, and that the party is the state and the state is the party."[81] The following year Nkrumah won a national plebiscite that provided for Ghana to become a Republic, with the prime minister position being abolished and replaced with a much more powerful president, who would be both head of government and head of state. Nkrumah contested the presidential race, and his opponent was his rival J. B. Danquah of the United Party. Nkrumah won the election, and was accorded the enhanced powers by the republican constitution. This constitution gave him power over the judiciary, whereby he could dismiss and replace the chief justice, and members of the judicial service and the police force. He made frequent use of these dictatorial powers.[82]

Nkrumah continued to increase his control over the public. In 1961 he created the Ghana Young Pioneers, a youth organization that would replace the Boy Scouts (which Nkrumah believed was imperialist and neo-colonialist). The members of the Young Pioneers were encouraged to report their parents or teachers if these adults expressed anti-Nkrumahist sentiment.[83] Meanwhile, a personality cult formed around Nkrumah, and he took on an honorific title: "His High Dedication, the Osagyefo Dr. Kwame Nkrumah."[84] The term Osagyefo translates to "a savior at war,"[85] which is a messianic title used for traditional rulers (chiefs). Nkrumah himself was not a chief, nor did he possess an earned doctorate. He had an honorary doctorate from his alma mater Lincoln University, a school that has never had a curriculum leading to an earned doctorate.

The republican constitution allowed Nkrumah to retain the PDA, which he used liberally. Among those arrested were his political rival J. B. Danquah and lawyer and politician Emmanuel Obetsebi Lamptey.

Both men died while being held in Ghana's notorious Nsawam Prison.[86] Though Nkrumah's most prominent opponent was now eliminated, he still did not wish to risk losing an election, so he cancelled elections that had been scheduled for 1965. Those elections were to expand the size of the parliament from 104 to 198 members. After elections were cancelled, the Central Committee of the CPP filled the seats, making Ghana, in effect, a one-party state with the "*Osagyefo*" at the helm.[87] As Nkrumah led Ghana down the thorny path of authoritarianism, he came under increasing criticism both domestically and internationally. Nevertheless, he retained the loyalty of many of the members of the African-American community, which by then numbered approximately 300.[88] Maya Angelou wrote the following about how the African-American expatriates felt about Nkrumah:

> We shadowed Nkrumah's every move, and read carefully his speeches, committing the more eloquent passages to memory. We recounted good gossip about him, loving his name, and furiously denied all negative rumors.[89]

Kevin Gaines stated that the repatriates were less concerned about the increasing diminishment of rights than they were about protecting Nkrumah and his regime. Nkrumah even had the strong support of Julian Wright Herve. Though her father, Richard, had voiced his concern about Nkrumah's stride toward Marxism, and had not been invited to the independence celebration, Herve remained a steadfast supporter of Nkrumah.[90] The expatriate community was so protective of Nkrumah that when one from their ranks was being deported, the others refused to assist him. Professor Wendell Pierre was accused of being a CIA agent, as were other Americans living in Ghana. But with Pierre there was no evidence to support such an accusation. Despite the dearth of evidence, Nkrumah ordered his termination from his position at the University, and his deportation. The African-American community did not support Pierre.[91]

While the repatriate community, as a whole, maintained its dedication to Nkrumah, that allegiance was by no means unanimous. One prominent repatriate, civil rights attorney Pauli Murray, publicly objected to the PDA,[92] and she was also dismayed by the anti-U.S. sentiments of Nkrumah's government. She became supportive of the opposition, while she also opposed those African Americans who continued to support

Nkrumah.[93] When eight members of the opposition were detained under the PDA, Murray assisted their counsel, who was none other than J. B. Danquah.[94] One African-American expatriate whom Murray considered as her "loyal friend and ally" was Joyce Markham, secretary to the director of the Law school. Though Markham was married to a Ghanaian who had worked in the Nkrumah government, she became very critical of the regime.[95] Bill Sutherland, who worked in Ghana's Finance Ministry, personally expressed to Nkrumah his opposition to the PDA, but obviously it was to no avail.[96] A dedicated pacifist, Sutherland founded Ghanaian chapters of the Fellowship of Reconciliation and the War Resisters League, two U.S.-based organizations that advocated nonviolence. He became dismayed by Nkrumah's refusal to embrace nonviolence. A disillusioned Sutherland left Ghana in 1961.[97]

Despite their loyalty to Nkrumah, many Black Americans faced the same problem of Professor Pierre: they fell under suspicion and had to defend themselves against accusations that they were agents of the U.S. Central Intelligence Agency. Some CPP government officials were wary of Black Americans, and there were some signs around Accra saying, "Beware of Afro-Americans." Persons whom Americans suspected to be CPP spies appeared at the University of Ghana to monitor the classes taught by African Americans. Leslie Lacy, who was teaching political science at the University of Ghana, also fell into disfavor with some of the Ghanaian Nkrumahists on campus. He described an incident where a student whom he believed was a "stooge" for the CPP came into his office and spoke to him in a most disrespectful manner. The student told Lacy, "You should be grateful that we let you Afro-Americans stay here, for if I were running things, I'd put all of you out." To that Lacy replied, "Your country? Well, Mr. Informer, let me tell you that this is my country too. My ancestors did not ask to leave here. More than likely, your ancestors did the selling. Now I'm back, and I have just as much right to be here as you have. NOW LEAVE!"[98] African Americans were either suspected of being CIA agents, or they were resented because of their access to President Nkrumah and the influential positions they held in Ghana.[99]

The growing opposition to the Nkrumah regime became so intense that there were numerous unsuccessful attempts on his life. The list of would-be assassins included members of the Ghanaian armed forces and the Ghanaian police force. These attempts left the president increasingly paranoid and progressively repressive. His distrust of the armed forces and police led him to create his own military force, which was called the President's Own Guard Regiment (POGR).[100] He also placed the military services under his direct control.[101] He dismissed two high-ranking major generals, including Joseph Arthur Ankrah, the commander of the army.[102] This action made Nkrumah despised among certain elements of the country's armed forces. What further angered many service members were rumors that his government provided more facilities for the POGR than for the established military.

## The 1966 Coup Makes African Americans Vulnerable

Finally, on February 24, 1966, while Nkrumah was away on a visit to China, his government was overthrown by a military coup led by the army and the national police force. After seizing power, the junta called itself the "National Liberation Council" (quite similar in name to the disbanded Ashanti opposition party, the "National Liberation Movement"), and named ousted general Joseph A. Ankrah as its chairman.[103] The junta quickly consolidated its control over the country and began reversing many of the actions taken by the CPP regime. Among those actions that were reversed was the invitation to African Americans. As Ronald Walters writes, the Politicals had seen Ghana as a base from which they could fight a war against racism in the U.S., but the purpose of the coup was to eliminate that African-American base of anti-Western propaganda.[104] The "Du Bois Avenue" sign on the campus of the University of Ghana was destroyed and the street renamed. Feeling suddenly unwelcome, many of the Politicals, such as Leslie Lacy, took it upon themselves to flee the suddenly hostile country. Within months after the coup, most had left, either voluntarily or involuntarily.[105] The NLC gave the Black foreigners little time to leave their ancestral and adopted homeland. One Jamaican woman, who had lived in Ghana for ten years, said the following about her forced exit from Ghana:

> Ghana security people . . . hand-delivered a letter that we had 24 hours to leave the country, myself and my eight-year-old daughter. . . . They were declaring other expatriates persona non grata. I would have continued serving Ghana. I became a refugee. I left all my goods and chattel, and I was not permitted to go back. . . . It was 25 years before I could return to Ghana, though I frequented other parts of Africa.[106]

The well-known repatriates were not spared the indignities described above. Shirley Graham Du Bois, was placed under house arrest and then deported. Her protégé, William Gardner Smith, who headed Ghana TV, was also detained and forced out of the country. Julia Wright Herve and her husband, whose journal had become the voice of the leftmost elements of the CPP, was deported. Dr. Alphaeus Hunton, who was continuing Dr. Du Bois's work on *Encyclopedia Africana*, along with his wife, was deported. The two settled in Zambia, where they were warmly received by President Kenneth Kaunda, a supporter of Nkrumah.[106] Maya Angelou, Julian Mayfield, Pauli Murray, and Bill Sutherland left prior to the coup. The latter two were disillusioned with the CPP government. Some of the exiles went to Tanzania, where they were welcomed by President Julius Nyerere. Mississippi-based civil rights activist Bob Moses, of the Student Non-violent Coordinating Committee, and his wife Dona Edwards had been planning to join the repatriate community in Ghana, but because of the coup they relocated to Tanzania instead. Nkrumah was given asylum in Guinea, where his friend Sekou Toure was the head of state. Toure gave Nkrumah the title of "Co-president," and Nkrumah resided there until he died in 1972. He was never allowed to return to Ghana.

Kwame Nkrumah's fate was similar to that of other African leaders who ushered in independence. During Nkrumah's nine-year tenure as head of state, twenty-eight African countries (including Ghana) gained their independence from colonial powers.[108] The majority of the heads of these fledgling nations attempted to consolidate their power and severely restrict opposition. Thirteen of these increasingly authoritarian leaders (including Nkrumah) were ousted in coups d'état. That was a pattern than existed in much of Africa for the next quarter of a century, a pattern that was not reversed until the early 1990s. In that wave of democratization in Africa, Ghana was once again a trendsetter.

2

# From Republic to Regime

## Ghana under the National Liberation Council

From 1966 to 1981 there were five more successful coups in Ghana, and each of the juntas gave themselves noble-sounding names. The original NLC was ousted in a palace coup in 1969, followed by three years of a civilian regime under Prime Minister Kofi Abrefa Busia. Busia was overthrown by a junta that called itself the "National Redemption Council," which later changed its name to the "Supreme Military Council" (SMC). The SMC was ousted in 1978 by a palace coup that brought in the SMC II. The SMC II was ousted in 1978 by the "Armed Forces Revolutionary Council" (AFRC). Three months later the AFRC handed over power to an elected government, but two years later it ousted the government, and established the "Provisional National Defence Council" (PNDC).

The pull factor that had lured African Americans to Ghana disappeared with the February 1966 coup. Ghana no longer had a head of state who welcomed African Americans. The NLC would not tolerate the presence of dissidents from the very country that had backed their takeover of the government. The ruling junta was so strongly pro-U.S. that it initially supported the U.S.'s involvement in the civil war in Vietnam,[1] a position not shared by other African countries. The NLC was right-wing in ideology, dictatorial in policy, and repressive in the implementation of those policies. One year after seizing power, the junta was challenged by a group of radical junior officers who were trying to overthrow the regime. The NLC prevailed, and the alleged coup leaders were taken before a firing squad and publicly executed.[2] Meanwhile the junta arbitrarily passed laws that eroded the public's personal liberties.

In October 1966 the regime made it a crime for the press to air statements that might "cause 'disaffection' against the NLC, the police or the armed forces." Those who violated the law could face up to three years of imprisonment.[3]

The NLC faced another armed challenge in April 1967, when a group of junior officers made an unsuccessful attempt to overthrow the regime. The fighting that ensued led to the death of one of the NLC members, General E. G. Kotoka.[4] Ghana's major airport is now named after General Kotoka. In February 1968 there was another coup attempt, this one led by Air Vice-Marshall Michael Otu, the chief of defense staff for the Ghana Armed forces. That insurrection also failed, but the chaos continued, along with dissatisfaction with NLC rule. In 1969, J. A. Ankrah (now a lieutenant general) was removed as Chairman and replaced by Brigadier Akwasi Afrifa.

The NLC did, however, allow a constitution to be drawn up for a proposed Second Republic. The constitution provided for a Westminster-style government, with a prime minister as head of government and a ceremonial president as head of state. Elections were scheduled for 1969, and the partisan alliances mirrored the ethnic divisions that plagued Ghana. Kofi Abrefa Busia, who had run for Prime Minister against Kwame Nkrumah back in 1956, was running again as the head of the Progress Party. The Progress Party was a new name for two old parties: the National Liberation Movement (from the 1956 election) and J. B. Danquah's United Party (from the 1960 election). The Progress Party represented what came to be called the "Danquah/Busia Tradition." The other tradition in Ghana, the "Nkrumahist Tradition," was to be represented by a party called the People's Popular Party, which was formed to continue the work of Nkrumah. That party, however, was banned by the junta.[5] With the People's Popular Party banned, the main opposition to the Progress Party was the National Alliance of Liberals, led by Komla Gbedemah, who had been Nkrumah's finance minister until he fell out of favor with the Osagyefo. Gbedemah worked to command the support of those Ghanaians who were loyal to the Nkruhamist tradition. The old split between the Danquah/Busiasts and the Nkrumahists resurfaced, but this time the two competing parties did not have strong ideological differences. The NAL was not willing to embrace the socialist economic plans and the stridently anti-West rhetoric of Nkrumah. Both major party platforms spoke of a need for rural development, for promoting Ghanaian business enterprises, for building more roads, hospitals, improving educational opportunities, and attracting more foreign investment.[6]

The election was held on August 29, 1969, and the results demonstrated that ethnicity, not ideology, had indeed become the basis of Ghana's political cleavage structure. Dr. Busia and his Progress Party won in a landslide, due to the high level of support that they received in the Akan regions of Ghana. The Akans overwhelmingly voted for Busia, while Gbedemah, an Ewe, won the lion's share of the votes in the Ewe-dominated Volta Region. The Volta Region was the only region carried by the NAL, and in that region they won 14 of the 16 parliamentary seats. The two that they lost were in Akan areas of the Volta Region. In the Akan regions of Ghana, the Progress Party won all of the seats in the Ashanti, Brong-Ahafo, and Central Regions, 10 of the 13 seats in the Western Region, and 14 of the 18 seats in the Eastern Region. The four seats that the NAL won in the Eastern Region were in non-Akan constituencies, while 2 of the 3 seats the Progress Party lost in the Western Region were in Akan districts, but they were dominated by the Nzima Tribe, which is Nkrumah's tribe. Those three seats went to neither the NAL nor the Progress Party, but to minor parties.[7] The 1969 election showed how much Ghana had devolved into an ethnically polarized state. The Ewes were now the stronghold of the Nkrumahists, with the Danquah/Busiaists having their strengths among the Akans. The Akan group where the Danquah/Buisaists received the largest number of votes was the Ashantis. The other Akan groups leaned Danquah/Busiast, but their votes could not be taken for granted. In 1969 the battleground regions were the non-Akan/non-Ewe territories. The largest group falling into the non-Akan/non-Ewe category was the Ga tribe, whose members dominated the area surrounding Accra, the capital and largest city. Like other African capital cities, Accra was populated by migrants from other regions of the country. Therefore many residents of Accra are Akans, who live among the indigenous Ga people. Greater Accra has now become a polyglot region that is liable to vote in either direction in elections, making it a battleground area. In 1969 there were nine seats in the Greater Accra region, and only three went to the Progress Party, three to the NAL, and three to minor parties.

## The Second Republic

The two most polarized of the larger ethnic groups are the Ashantis and the Ewes. The Ashantis and their allies from other Akan groups comprise nearly half of Ghana's population. Between these Akan groups, and the moderate support from non-Akan/non-Ewe regions, the Progress Party was able to score a victory in 1969. That is how elections in Ghana have been since that time. Candidates running in the Danquah/Busia tradition have held onto their support in the Ashanti region, and have won when they were able to secure support from other Akan groups and make inroads among the Gas and other non-Ewe/non-Akan ethnic groups. During the Fourth Republic, the Northern Region has become a stronghold of the major party that presents itself as the heir to the Nkrumah tradition. However, the small population of that region has sometimes been insufficient to offset the Danquah/Busiaist strength among the Ashantis and other Akan groups.

International observers deemed the 1969 election to be "Free and Fair," but the subsequent Second Republic was less than democratic. When the Akan-dominated regime took office in 1969, it tried to purge from government employment persons from ethnic groups whom they did not deem as loyal to the Regime. The Progress Party sought to amend the constitution and allow the government to fire, after six months, any official appointed by the NLC. Between March and April, 568 officials were fired, most being Ewes and Gas. The Busia regime also targeted foreigners, which did not bode well for those few Black Americans remaining in Ghana, or for those with hopes of returning now that civilian rule had been restored. Immediately after assuming office, the Progress Party parliament passed an Aliens Compliance Order, requiring aliens without work permits to obtain them within two weeks or leave the country. Then in June 1970, the government passed the Ghana Business (Promotion) Act. This was an enhancement to the NLC's Ghanaian Enterprises Decree, which required that, within five years, many small businesses in Ghana should be reserved for nationals. The Progress Party's Aliens Compliance Order took it a step further by expanding the range of small businesses that aliens would not be allowed to own in Ghana.[8] There would be no invitation of Black Americans to repatriate to the Motherland, as there had been during the days of Kwame Nkrumah.

Prime Minister Busia did not wish to reinstate Nkrumah-era policies, and he continued in the NLC's mission to eradicate the memory of Ghana's first president. Busia was able to get parliament to pass a bill banning the selling and public display of photographs of Nkrumah. In addition, parliament made it a criminal offense to mention Nkrumah's name.[9] In 1971, when the pro-Nkrumah People's Popular Party was inaugurated in Kumasi, with its followers singing old CPP songs, the government banned the party. The government also passed legislation criminalizing the promotion of the restoration of Kwame Nkrumah.[10] Busia also cracked down on the press, something his followers had accused the Nkrumah administration of doing. When Busia called for dialogue with the White minority racist apartheid regime in South Africa, he was criticized by Cameron Duodo, editor of the government-owned *Daily Graphic*. Busia responded by firing Duodo.[11]

The Progress Party government escaped the opprobrium of contemporary international observers, but the repressive measures during the Second Republic would face strong condemnation were they to be implemented in today's post-Cold War world. Since 2006 *The Economist* has published a "Democracy Index" that rates the world's regimes on the basis of their adherence to democratic principles. The three categories used in the index are "full democracy," "flawed democracy," "hybrid regime," and "authoritarian."[12] Ghana under Busia would qualify as a "hybrid regime" at best, and this would hurt its standing among donor nations of the West.

Though the Busia regime avoided international criticism, it did not escape domestic criticism, but it perhaps might have had the economy been noticeably improving during the years of the Second Republic. Throughout the world there are repressive regimes that retain popularity among the masses because the regimes have brought about appreciable economic improvements. Persons living in impoverished countries prioritize physiological needs over civil liberties. As Abraham Maslow observed when studying human psychology, "if an organism is dominated by the physiological needs, all other needs may become simply non-existent or be pushed into the background."[13] Unfortunately for Busia, Ghana's economy was in terrible shape. The rate of unemployment was at 50 percent. To make economic matters worse, the country was so deep in debt that it was paying out more for debt servicing than it was receiving in foreign aid.[14] There were also drastic increases in prices for basic items, and there were commodity shortages due to import restrictions imposed by the government. The Progress Party also imposed a "National Development Levy" on all incomes above $980 (US), and university students were required to begin paying for their upkeep or take out government loans. These measures were imposed to help pay the country's short-term debt, which was due in less than a year. That debt was as high as the import bill for half a year.[15] Ghana teetered on bankruptcy, and its economy was at the mercy of the International Monetary Fund (IMF), which required the country to devalue its currency by 48 percent.[16] In less than four years, the cedi, the unit of currency, had been devalued twice.[17]

The economic situation in the country led to a drastic decline in the popularity of the Busia regime. The dissatisfaction with the government reached into the ranks of the military. Members of the military forces were upset over an austerity budget that slashed military expenditures by nearly 25 percent.[18] Perhaps the angriest among those in the armed forces were middle-ranking officers. Some felt that they had been denied promotions because of their disassociation from politics or because of their ethnicity. The latter feeling was shared by many Ewe officers.[19] On January 13, 1972, a group of middle-ranking officers, led by Colonel Ignatius Acheampong, seized power and deposed Busia and his parliament. The junta called itself the "National Redemption Council" (NRC). The original members included the seven leaders of the coup (majors and lieutenant colonels) and one civilian, E. N. Moore, who, ten years earlier, had served as the defense counsel in a trial of persons accused of attempting to assassinate Kwame Nkrumah. Though Acheampong was an Ashanti, the members of the junta came from diverse ethnic backgrounds, with Ewes having a higher percentage than their percentage in the general population.[20]

## The NRC/SMC Years

Though Acheampong overthrew a government that was of the Danquah/Busia tradition, he was not in the rivaling Nkrumahist tradition. In an interview with *Africa* magazine, Acheampong denounced both Busia and Nkrumah, and stated his support for the coup that had toppled Nkrumah six years earlier.[21] Upon seizing power, Danquah declared that he was neither an Nkrumahist nor a Busiaist. In another interview conducted one month after seizing power, Acheampong was asked if he preferred Nkrumah or Busia. He replied, "I will choose neither of the two. I have my own line of conduct, which I follow. Their time is past."[22] However, in a radical departure from the policy of the Second Republic, the NRC abandoned Busia's policy of holding dialogue with the virulently racist and violent White minority regime in South Africa.[23] In the *Africa* magazine interview, Acheampong said that his NRC government "rejects any form of dialogue with apartheid South Africa, as long as that country sticks to its policy of racism."[24]

While condemning racism in South Africa, Acheampong was no champion of democracy in Ghana. His junta disbanded the Second Republic and the constitution that had given life to that Republic. Whatever civil liberties were guaranteed under the constitution were no longer protected under the NRC. In May 1972 the Council issued a "Defamation by Newspapers Decree," which allowed the government to jail journalists and their editors for writing articles critical of the NRC.[25] These measures were taken in the climate of a declining economy. There were shortages of basic commodities, and consumers had to wait in long lines for products such as rice, sugar, flour, and tinned goods. This encouraged hoarding and sales on the black market. Prices skyrocketed, and Ghana was rated as having the second-highest inflation rate in the world. One cause for the continuous increase in prices was a practice that Ghanaians refer to as "kalabule." This involves business owners (both large and small) hoarding products that people relied heavily on. After the goods were accumulated into the hands of a small number of market owners, the owners would sell them at extremely high prices.[26] The consumers could barely afford to pay the prices, but they had little choice, as many of the overpriced commodities were necessary for a household. Kalabule was rampant during the days of the NRC. Widespread corruption fostered the continuance of kalabule because in order to purchase the goods, the distributors needed to receive "chits" granting them the right to buy the products. The government issued the chits, which is where corruption entered. Certain market owners received chits as favors, and they then hoarded the products, to be sold at a price high above the market rate. The NRC days are remembered as times of economic scarcity and political repression.

The Acheampong regime came under criticism, but its response was to increase its hold on government. Colonel Acheampong became General Acheampong, and he replaced the NRC with the "Supreme Military Council" (SMC). This body included the inspector general of the police and the commanders of all of the branches of the military. This revised regime was now called "Union Government," or "UNIGOV." The UNIGOV constitution that Acheampong forced on Ghanaians was one that increased the role of the military and made no provisions to respect the right to dissent. When university students demonstrated, the government closed down all three universities, and when physicians voiced their support of a strike by other professionals, armed soldiers stormed into the country's main hospital and forcibly ejected the doctors.[27] There was also physical harassment of those who were opposed to the very existence of UNIGOV.

Facing mounting domestic criticism, the SMC agreed to hold a referendum on UNIGOV, scheduled for March 30, 1978. Voting was held, but when the earliest vote counts showed UNIGOV going down to defeat, General Acheampong confiscated all polling boxes and had the ballots secretly counted. It was then announced that UNIGOV won with 55.6 percent of the vote. Some of the organizations opposed to UNIGOV were poised to launch protests, but Acheampong prevented this by banning their organizations and arresting opponents of UNIGOV.[28]

On July 5, 1978, General Acheampong, Chairman of the Supreme Military Council, was deposed in a palace coup. He was replaced by Lt. General Fred Akuffo, a member of the SMC. This elite-motivated change did not improve the reputation of the SMC. After taking over, Akuffo devalued the currency and implemented an austerity budget. The response of the public was a wave of strikes. When workers at the state-owned electricity corporation went out on strike, Gen. Akuffo imposed a state of emergency and began dismissing workers. Unable to gain public support for the SMC, Akuffo announced that political parties could form, and that there would be elections in June 1979. By April of that year there were six parties eligible to contest the election, but the two major parties were the People's National Party, which was Nkrumahist, and the Popular Front Party, which was in the Danquah/Busia tradition.[29] Gocking states that, "The vagueness of their platforms was indicative of how much they both attempted to offer all things to all people."[30] As was the situation with the Second Republic, the Third Republic would not see major ideological differences between the two major parties.

## The Rawlings Era

On May 15, 1979, one month before the scheduled election, Ghana endured another coup attempt. The leader of this rebellion was an Ewe air force lieutenant by the name of Jerry John Rawlings. Though the attempt failed, Rawlings became an immediate hero among his fellow junior officers in the Ghanaian military. On June 4, a group of soldiers from the rank-and-file stormed into the prison where Lt. Rawlings was held and released him. After a brief battle with forces loyal to the SMC, Rawlings and his junior officers seized control of the government and named themselves the "Armed Forces Revolutionary Council" (AFRC), with Rawlings appointed as Chairman. The new junta's rationale for seizing power was that the SMC had done nothing to root out corruption in the ranks of the military, but they also shared the public's anger at the rampant kalabule taking place in the markets. The AFRC was very public in their tackling these two issues. They arrested a number of top military officers and placed them before tribunals, where they were pronounced guilty and rapidly sentenced. Eight of the officers whom the AFRC pronounced as "guilty" were summarily executed by firing squads. Among those arrested and executed were three former heads of state: General Acheampong and his successor General Akuffo, and General Akwasi Afrifa from the NLC days.[31] The junta was also quite brutal in their efforts to end kalabule. Many of Ghana's market women were placed under arrest by the AFRC and subjected to the junta's abbreviated makeshift trial system. Hoarded goods were confiscated and sold to the public at drastically reduced prices. Those who were judged guilty of hoarding were publicly stripped and beaten. The AFRC also went after the market women's wealthy benefactors, most of whom were Lebanese. Soldiers ransacked shops; they looted and distributed the stolen goods to the public.[32] These actions often had the strong approval of the Ghanaian public, who had put up with years of shortages, inflation, and kalabule. Chairman Rawlings became immensely popular,[33] which could have been a temptation for him to remain in power. Nevertheless, he promised that elections for the Third Republic would proceed as previously planned.

The elections were held in July 1979, and the two major contenders were an Ashanti named Victor Owusu, of the Popular Front Party (PFP), and Dr. Hilla Limman, a northerner, of the People's National Party (PNP). The PFP was in the Danquah/Busia tradition, while the PNP was in the Nkrumahist tradition. The PNP won 71 of the 140 seats in parliament, giving it an absolute majority, and Limman received only a plurality of votes in the presidential race. According to the provisions of the new constitution, if a president did not receive a majority of votes in the first round, the first- and second-place finishers would have to compete in a runoff. Owusu came in second to Limman, so the two contested the second round. This time Limman received 62 percent of the vote, and he was declared the winner.[34] On September 24, 1979, Lt. Rawlings stepped down, and Limman assumed the office of the presidency.[35]

Though the PNP proclaimed itself to be a Nkrumahist party, the Limman administration did not have a coherent ideology. Limman's goal was development, and, unlike Nkrumah, he was not committed to a socialist path to achieve that objective. There were many obstacles in Limman's way. Ghana's chief export, cocoa, was experiencing declining prices; the roads were in terrible condition, as was Ghana's rail system; inflation rose to over 100 percent, and kalabule made an unwelcome return.[36] To top this off, the Limman administration faced ethnic challenges from Ewes, who felt excluded from the government, and from Akans, who had never supported his administration.[37] Being a northerner, Limman was vulnerable to criticism from both rivaling groups. Limman's government proved unable to meet the challenges, and opposition was flourishing.

One source of the opposition was from the very person who had handed the reins of power to Limman: Flight Lieutenant Jerry Rawlings. Rawlings was still popular among civilians and among a large faction of the military. On December 31, 1981, just two years into the Third Republic, Limman was toppled by a coup led by Rawlings. Rawlings quickly solidified his power over Ghana, and he suspended parliament and outlawed all political parties.[38]

This second Rawlings-led junta named itself the "Provisional National Defense Council" (PNDC), with Rawlings as the Chairman. At the outset, the PNDC took a left-wing posture. They established "Workers' Defense Committees" to oversee working conditions in factories and other workplaces, and "People's Defense Committees" that did likewise in urban and rural communities. These committees were modeled after similar organizations in Cuba and Libya.[39]

The PNDC proclaimed itself to be at the vanguard of a people's revolution. There was an outpouring of support from students and from the masses on the street, while those in the middle classes were deemed to be enemies of the revolution.[40] With this fervor came some of the abuses that had been seen during the AFRC days. Three high-court judges, who had overturned rulings from the AFRC, were kidnapped and murdered on June 30, 1982. Though no members of the PNDC were convicted of these murders, some Ghanaians believed that the junta was responsible. Eventually five men (soldiers and former soldiers) were tried and found guilty, and three of them were executed by firing squads. The trials were as haphazardly conducted as those that found guilty the top members of the military during the AFRC days. Meanwhile there were plots and attempts to overthrow the PNDC government, each one thwarted. One of the main sources of contention among the plotters was the belief that the Ewes, Rawlings's ethnic group, were wielding excessive influence over the country under PNDC rule.[41]

World history and African history in particular provide examples that make it clear that in order for a coup to develop into a stable government, there must be economic progress. The dire condition of Ghana's economy made possible the June 1979 and December 1981 coups d'état. Thus, it was imperative that Chairman Rawlings address economic issues. Initially the PNDC was a left-leaning junta that praised Kwame Nkrumah. Rawlings turned to left-wing countries for assistance: Cuba, Libya, and the Soviet Union. These countries, however, were not able to provide the amount of aid that Ghana needed, so in 1983 Rawlings performed an ideological about-face and turned to the capitalist nations and their international financial institutions (the World Bank and the IMF).[42] These institutions imposed conditions for the receipt of their assistance, which required the PNDC to impose a structural adjustment program. Ghana adopted an austerity budget that required a devaluation of the cedi, privatization of public enterprises, the elimination of subsidies on food and fuel, abandonment of import substitution, the implementation of user fees for education, health care and utilities, and drastic reduction of spending on social services.[43] Rawlings had adopted a program similar to those advocated by then-current right-wing world leaders Ronald Reagan of the United States and Margaret Thatcher of the United Kingdom in their respective countries. However, Rawlings himself never publicly joined the ranks of rightist Western leaders. Though he came to power nearly a decade before the fall of Communism in Eastern Europe, he never embraced the Cold War that was at the time being fought by the U.S. and the U.K. Nor did Rawlings become an ethnic chauvinist, such as Jean-Marie Le Pen of France and Pym Fortuyn of the Netherlands. Rawlings never completely severed his ties from revolutionary movements. He strongly opposed the apartheid regime in South Africa, maintained ties with Cuba, and he bolstered the image of self-proclaimed Marxist Kwame Nkrumah.[44] Nevertheless, under his PNDC Ghana became a developmental dictatorship, such as was seen in other Third World countries such as Chile, Taiwan, and South Korea, where the ruling juntas utilized their absolute power in order to impose unpopular austerity programs.

The economic recovery program appears to have produced some of the desired results. Between 1982 and 1992 profits from Ghana's timber industry had a nearly tenfold increase, and from 1983 to 1985 there was a more than 90 percent decline in the rate of inflation. Ghana's gross national product rose from .7 percent in 1983 to 5.5 in 1985.[45] The economic recovery program continued through the 1980s, and the policies led to the end of Ghana's economic decline, replaced by a period of growth. The coup attempts of the early 1980s had come to an end, and in 1992 the PNDC announced that they would usher in Democracy. They lifted their control over the press, unbanned political parties, and scheduled parliamentary and presidential elections for the end of year. The PNDC reformed itself into a political party, calling itself the NDC (National Democratic Congress), with Rawlings as the candidate. Their primary competitors were the Danquah/Busia party, now called the New Patriotic Party (NPP). There were some smaller Nkrumahist parties, but most Nkrumahists among the populace tended to flock to the NDC, despite that party's radical departure from the economic policies of Kwame Nkrumah.

The 1992 elections occurred in two rounds. The first round, in November, was for the presidential race, and the second round, in December, was for parliamentary seats. The presidential elections proceeded as scheduled, but not without controversy. There were some irregularities, and there were allegations of voter suppression. The NPP alleged that there was voter suppression in their stronghold, the Ashanti Region, and that there was over-voting in the Ewe-dominated Volta Region, which was Rawlings's base of power. Rawlings was declared the winner, but the NPP contested that result on the basis of the allegations. International observers acknowledged that there were irregularities, but they asserted that this did not affect the final outcome of the presidential race.[46]

There were indeed irregularities in the 1992 election. Members of the London-based Commonwealth Observers Group, who helped monitor the election, heard complaints that the ruling PNDC misused state resources for party campaigning purposes.[47] In a rally launching the NDC, a large number of civil servants were alleged to have attended in their government vehicles. Moreover, the state-owned buses were reported to have ferried party loyalists to the rally. The opposition also claimed that the incumbent government provided itself a great deal of exposure on the state-controlled television and radio stations.[48] The Commonwealth Observers Group also reported that on election day new polling places had been established, which led many to appear at the wrong polling place, sometimes after waiting for hours to vote.[49] Yakubu Saaka examined the allegations of a stolen election. Looking at census projections, he discovered that in four constituencies in the Volta Region—the NDC's stronghold—voter turnout exceeded 100 percent of the eligible population.[50] One journalist estimated that there were two million "ghost voters" who came out on election day to assist Rawlings.[51] This is believed to have been done by double-voting and under-age voting. The opposition party (the NPP) cited 33 constituencies in which minors impersonated dead persons so that they could vote in the election.[52] There were also reports of elections officials failing to properly seal the ballot boxes and failing to follow other stipulated procedures.[53]

Less than one decade after the election, I interviewed a number of prominent Ghanaians about the 1992 elections. One NPP Member of Parliament from the Ashanti Region (an NPP stronghold) said that on election day soldiers were patrolling the streets and wielding firearms. A member of Ghana's Electoral Commission told me that there were reports that on election day the government amassed troops in the Ashanti Region, and that civilian security forces intimidated NPP officials who were campaigning in the Volta Region. He also said that there were allegations that in the Eastern Region (another NPP stronghold), there was outright changing of votes. An NPP member of parliament told me that me that there were reports of youths as young as eleven years old illegally casting votes in the Volta Region.[54]

Despite allegations such as those listed above, international observers validated the first round of the elections, which awarded the victory to Lt. Jerry Rawlings. The NPP did not accept this conclusion, so they boycotted the December parliamentary elections. As a result, Rawlings and the NDC were able to govern without parliamentary opposition, but they allowed other parties to develop and exist.

Elections were held again in 1996, and Rawlings ran for a second elected term. This time the NPP contested the presidential and parliamentary elections. They did not prevail in the presidential elections, nor did they overcome the NDC's majority in parliament, but they accepted the results and became the official opposition. With a vibrant opposition and a free press, Ghana had made the transition to democracy. It now had one of the most stable governments in Africa, and the most stable in West Africa. It had also become an attractive destination for tourists. Ghana was also one of the countries that set the trend for the rest of

Sub-Saharan Africa. At the beginning of the decade of the 1990s countries in Africa were beginning this trend of holding multi-party elections and subsequently discarding military regimes. At the start of 1992, the year Ghana began its transition, only 10 countries in Africa allowed multi-party elections. Since then 22 more countries on that continent have held multi-party elections.[55] Ghana was on the crest of this wave.

# 3

# From Regime to Republic

## Democracy Under Rawlings

In 1993, the first year of the Fourth Republic, the Rawlings government launched the Ministry of Tourism. Through that ministry, the NDC government touted its Nkrumah-style pan-Africanism to attract African Americans to Ghana as their vacation destination. The previous year, in 1992, the government held its first "PANAFEST," a cultural festival that coincides with Emancipation Day (August 1), the day in 1833 when the British outlawed slavery in their Caribbean colonies. It was apparently lost on the creators of the festival that for thirty-two years after the day that they commemorate, the ancestors of many of the people whom they hoped to bring to Ghana to celebrate continued to suffer under the brutality of U.S. slavery. Nevertheless, the launching of the festival marked the beginning of attempts to bring African Americans to Ghana, along with their dollars. In 1995, Rawlings visited New York City and addressed an event called "Harlem salutes Jerry Rawlings." Rawlings told the mostly Black crowd that African Americans should "spend your vacations with us in Ghana and breathe deeply your roots, history and future," and to "invest in the economic and social future of Ghana."[1] Rawlings appeared to wish to take this invitation a step further. In a visit to the United States in February 1999, Rawlings announced that parliament would present a bill offering dual citizenship for Black Americans. He stated, "There's no reason why I will deny my fellow Black African the right to enjoy the citizenship as I enjoy as an African." Rawlings went on to say that, "It certainly won't hurt in trying to get more Americans in Ghana, and contributing to Ghana's future."[2]

At first glance it appears that Jerry Rawlings was reinstating the invitation that Kwame Nkrumah gave to African Americans to relocate to Ghana, an invitation that had lain dormant for three decades. There was, however, a major difference. Nkrumah invited African Americans to bring their expertise and help build a newly independent socialist state on the mother continent. Rawlings, on the contrary, wanted African Americans to bring their money, not their expertise, and contribute to the economy of this newly democratized neoliberal capitalist state. While both pan-African presidents wanted diasporic Africans to come from the U.S., Nkrumah wanted their technical and intellectual assistance, while Rawlings wanted their financial capital.

In 2000 Rawlings was unable to run for a third term, according to the stipulations placed in the constitution of the Fourth Republic. Elections were held near the end of that year, and the NDC was ousted from power. The opposing NPP won both the presidency and a majority of the seats in Parliament. In January 2001 Rawlings did something very rare in African Politics: he peacefully handed over power to his opposition. The new president, John Adgekum Kufuor, was an Ashanti of the Danquah/Busia tradition. Kufuor did not reach out to African Americans, as Rawlings had. Kufuor visited the U.S. in June 2001, and he met with President Bush. On June 27 he spoke to a packed audience at the Ghanaian embassy to the U.S. I was there to listen to the new president. He spoke of his desire for Ghanaian-born U.S. citizens to reinstate their Ghanaian passports and become citizens of both countries.[3] However, he did not say one word about African Americans being allowed to become dual citizens. That proposal died when the Rawlings presidency ended.

## The Quest for Dual Citizenship

Six years into his presidency, Kufuor's government finally launched a project to reach out to Diasporans. In 2007, Jake Obetsebi-Lamptey, the Minister of Tourism and Diasporan Relations, announced the creation of the "Joseph Project." The purpose of the project was to encourage descendants of the Atlantic slave trade to return to Ghana. Minister Lamptey boasted that, "Ghana is a beacon in Africa of good governance. . . . A natural inspiration for African pride."[4] Again the push was for investment, not assistance. Minister Obetsebi-Lamptey made the following written statement:

> A variety of land and home ownership schemes are being evolved that will allow Diasporans to have real ownership of a piece of the Homeland. These will range from symbolic plots, real ownership but of a very small piece of real estate, time share apartments and land for private development.[5]

One group of foreigners to whom the Kufuor Administration gave more substantial offers of land was White farmers from Zimbabwe, who had lost property during that country's land reform program. It must be noted that four other countries in tropical Africa also sent out invitations to White farmers from Zimbabwe. The purpose was to bolster the agricultural sector.[6]

Black Americans have heeded the call to come to Ghana, both to vacation and to invest. Historian Justin Williams traveled to Ghana in 2010 and met with African-American expatriates, just as I did six years later. One person whom he interviewed was Mona Boyd, a Black American woman from Boston, who is married to a Ghanaian. In 1993 Boyd moved to Ghana and started a company named "Land Tours Ghana." In 1998, during President Bill Clinton's historic tour to Ghana, Ms. Boyd served as his guide.[7] Boyd has taken advantage of the rapidly growing tourism industry in Ghana, and African Americans have contributed to that growth in no small way. Justin Williams concluded that, "Ghana has become the Africa black Americans want to see, impoverished, bustling, full of culture, but also defying racist stereotypes of African political and economic dysfunction."[8]

Williams's study makes detailed comparisons between the idealistic revolutionary socialism of Nkrumah, the president of the First Republic, and the pragmatic neoliberal capitalism of the presidents of the Fourth Republic. In so doing, he does interview several African Americans, but his aim was not to examine their opinions of the current Fourth Republic, or of their involvement in the country's politics. My study examines the same universe (African-American expatriates in Ghana), but my aim was to determine if they are in any way politically involved, as were their predecessors during the First Republic.

Three of the persons whom I interviewed shared the political philosophies of the first generation of "Politicals." They were affiliated with the All-African People's Revolutionary Party (AAPRP). The AAPRP is an organization that was first conceptualized by Kwame Nkrumah in 1968, while he was living in exile in Guinea.[9] The AAPRP was subsequently created and retains its reverence for Nkrumah. The organization is pan-Africanist and socialist, and has chapters in Africa and the United States.[10] Each of my three respondents who are affiliated with the AAPRP informed me that they had not been involved in politics in the U.S. One told me "I never voted, never was a member of a political party." Another said that in the U.S. "[t]here wasn't much difference between the parties." That person made the same observation about the two parties in Ghana. I mentioned to that respondent that the NDC is somewhat of an offshoot of Nkrumah's CPP and is now seen as the Nkrumahist party. I asked the respondent if this made the NDC more attractive to some on the left. To that the respondent said, "No, not at all. Now even the NPP praises Nkrumah." The first respondent said likewise about the parties in Ghana. That person expressed no preference for a political party in the U.S. or in Ghana. The response was "to me, it's all one big thing." When I asked if the respondent would vote in Ghana if given citizenship, the answer was, "I doubt it." A third respondent said that the current political structure in Ghana is a "façade of democracy that is modeled after the West." Like the other two AAPRP members, this respondent did not vote when living in the U.S. Another respondent, who has worked on projects with the AAPRP, said the following:

> Supporting one party or another: NEVER, not even when I was in the United States. I don't favor one party over another. I'm an Nkrumahist, but I don't get involved in politics. I don't know the difference between the NPP and the NDC. I did appreciate [NDC President] Atta Mills, but his presidency didn't make me look at politics at all.

The AAPRP members' assessment of Ghana's parties was shared by a respondent who was not a member of the organization. About Ghana's two major parties, this respondent said, "They are pretty much the same, and for that reason I don't have a preference. All of them are capitalistic. To me NPP or NDC is all the same." But unlike the AAPRP respondents, this person did vote back in the U.S., and was affiliated with the Democratic Party.

Two of the AAPRP respondents stated that they would become citizens of Ghana, if that were available to them, while one did not discuss the possibility of citizenship. That respondent did mention the effort to streamline the process of gaining a "right to abode," but is not personally involved in that effort. I asked another AAPRP respondent if there was a desire to become a Ghanaian citizen, and the answer was "Absolutely!" The third AAPRP respondent, when asked about the now-dormant proposal for dual citizenship, said, "I think that will be very good." This respondent expressed some disappointment over the fact that not even the Ghanaian-born children of expatriates are allowed to become citizens of the country of their birth.

Though the NDC returned to power in 2009, and held power for eight years, dual citizenship has not yet become available for African Americans. In October 2015, one year before the election that would bring the NPP back into power, that party's standard-bearer, Nana Akufo-Addo, was in the U.S. on a visit, along with an entourage. On October 21 he spoke to the Heritage Foundation, a conservative think tank.[11] Two days later, he met with a small group that included myself. I raised the issue of dual citizenship for African Americans living in Ghana. Akufo-Addo responded by saying, "They are a very productive group of people." Despite paying that compliment, he would not express any support for dual citizenship.

With the prospects dead for dual citizenship, also dead are the opportunities for African Americans to exercise the franchise in Ghana. This, however, does not prevent them from involvement in non-electoral political activities. Ghana under the Fourth Republic is very much a democracy, and being such, the citizens, non-citizen residents, and even the visitors have the freedom to participate in political campaigns, to voice their opinions orally and in writing, and even to become involved in peaceful protests. Similarly, prior to the passage of the Voting Rights Act in 1965, African Americans took advantage of the democratic protections enshrined in the U.S. Constitution and involved themselves in non-electoral political activities. Officials in the governments of Southern states, and discriminatory state and local laws precluded African Americans from voting in elections, but the protections of the Bill of Rights allowed them to participate in other political activities, and the Fourteenth Amendment prevented state officials from abridging these rights. Much of the Civil Rights Movement involved political activities other than voting.

The purpose of my interviews of expatriates is to determine if African Americans in Ghana are involved in similar activities, since voting is not an option available to them.

## Respondents' Assessments of Ghana's Political Parties

The data from the interviews shows that, though many of the respondents were politically active in the U.S., only a small number are politically involved in Ghana. One respondent, who is married to a Ghanaian, was involved in the U.S. with the well-known rights organization called the Children's Defense Fund, and was involved in what the respondent described as "children's rights issues." This respondent once worked in New York City on behalf of victims of police brutality and hate crimes, and was also involved with issues of concern to immigrants. This respondent was registered as a Democrat back in the United States, and worked on the staff of a U.S. senator, writing letters to constituents. In Ghana the respondent worked with Konadu Rawlings, the wife of the head of state. The respondent had the following to say about the work with the former First Lady of Ghana:

> When I first moved here, I did a bit of consulting. I even worked with Nana Rawlings on some women's issues. I consulted her on the "Sheroes Forum," and about girls' education.

The "Sheroes Forum" is a regularly scheduled event sponsored by the "Sheroes Foundation," an organization that promotes gender equality and female political empowerment.[12]

This respondent, however, was not altogether pleased about the state of politics in Ghana, stating that, "politics here tends to be about association and money, which is more blatant than back in Washington, D.C. . . . 'Dashing' in politics is acceptable here." "Dashing" is the term used for dissemination of money in return for favors.

Though this person was registered as a Democrat, the interviewee said, "I would say that I'm more independent. . . . I could go to the Republican Party one day if the issues make sense."

The above interviewee was very much involved in politics in the U.S. Only one respondent whom I spoke with was more involved. This extremely involved respondent became involved in politics back in high school, while attending a highly politicized private school. In 2008 the respondent was a high school student and was involved in Barack Obama's campaign for president. The respondent said, "I was in high school canvassing. I was bitterly disappointed that I couldn't vote." This respondent went on to attend a prestigious university in the U.S., had a column in the campus newspaper, and wrote about foreign policy and women's issues. As a student, the respondent became involved in the politics of the city where the university was located, as well as issues at the university, two of which were equal pay for women and sexual misconduct at the university. In addition to this, the respondent was involved with the organization for Black students at the university. As for electoral politics, the respondent worked in the office of a Democratic congresswoman. As for partisan identification, the respondent said, "I'm a Democrat by registration, but I'm independent," and contemplated voting in a Republican presidential primary for former Governor John Huntsman of Utah. This respondent has become involved in politics in Ghana. The respondent has written about language policy, sanitation issues, and "anything with local politics in Ghana." An area of particular concern to this respondent is a government proposal to replace English as the language of instruction in school, and replace it with the dominant Ghanaian language of each respective region. The respondent said, "I think that's silly." Non-Akans are also quite concerned about this proposed change, as it will discriminate against them. Many non-Akans have migrated into Akan-dominated regions of Ghana, so they will be hurt by the policy. It will also have negative implications for African-American expatriates, most of whom are not fluent in Ghanaian languages.

I interviewed someone else who was active as a student in the U.S. This respondent went to a predominantly White university, was involved with the school's organization for Black students, and served as an officer in that organization. The respondent was not politically active subsequent to college, but was affiliated with the Democratic Party. In Ghana the respondent leans more closely toward the NPP, upset about the declining value of the cedi during the Mahama Administration.

I met with another expatriate who was very much involved with political issues in Ghana. This individual said the following:

> I joined small groups in Accra and the Central and Northern Regions to do community development. As a non-citizen, I have no standing to testify. Xenophobia is alive, and I can

> understand where this xenophobia comes from. You must have the understanding that you're a visitor in this country.
>
> I've worked on doing process evaluation on national constitutional review committees. I worked with professors in social work and sociology on the National Health Insurance Scheme. There was a lot of scrutiny of me. I did work on field research, writing, and work on national issues. But I walk a fine line.

Considering all the issues that this respondent is involved in, and the scrutiny this individual receives as a foreigner, I asked if this respondent feels compelled to expand activism to include lobbying for dual citizenship. The following is the answer given to me:

> I would consider dual citizenship if it were available, but it's not one of my activism interests. But as it is right now, residence permits are expensive, running $1,000 per year. Also, the bureaucracy of a tax-clearance certification, going to immigration, picking up the papers. The low pay of the [government] workers doesn't give [them] much incentive to work. They often have jobs they can't get fired from. Bureaucracy moves slow, and the administrative process moves slow.

I asked the respondent's opinion about the parties in Ghana. The respondent said, "Here I support neither of the two parties. I live in a political neighborhood, but I stay out of politics. I have election fatigue here in Ghana. They are making everything a political issue." The respondent said the following when asked if the two parties in Ghana were different from one another:

> The NPP focuses on the Golden Age of Business. They're like the Republicans. The NDC calls themselves social democrats, and looks like the Democratic Party in the U.S. But I don't see a difference in quality of people's lives, no matter who is in control. I have witnessed growth, but I don't think it depends on which party is in control. There are so many politicians, but they all sound the same.

During the interview, the United States was in the midst of the 2016 presidential primaries. I asked if the respondent had a party preference in the U.S. The answer I received was a resounding "NO!" The respondent indicated a very strong preference for independent Senator Bernie Sanders, who was at that time running for the Democratic Party nomination for president. Sanders is a self-described socialist, who was running far to the left of the other candidates for president.

The above interviewee fell on the left of the U.S. political spectrum, as was the case with most of the respondents. While one of the previously discussed respondents indicated a possible preference for a Republican (John Huntsman), only one reported having actually worked on the campaign of a conservative Republican candidate for office. That respondent nevertheless claimed to be a "die-hard Democrat," but did campaign for a conservative Republican governor in a statewide race back in the U.S. Later on, however, this person supported Jesse Jackson's presidential campaign for the Democratic presidential nomination, but noted that, "I wouldn't say I actually worked on his campaign," as was the case with the Republican's gubernatorial campaign. The respondent also expressed support of a controversial left-leaning Black Democratic municipal officeholder in the U.S., one who was reviled by White Americans. The respondent said that this hated Black politician "Was a good guy. He was for the people. [With him] there was hope for Black folks." I asked this respondent to state a party preference in Ghana, and the respondent indicated a preference for the NPP. The respondent expressed dissatisfaction with the then-current NDC government under John Mahama. When comparing it with the previous NPP government under John Kufuor, the respondent had the following to say:

> It seems to me that when you can see what's been accomplished, there was less of a disparity between the cedi and the dollar under the NPP administration of Kufuor. Now it's 4-1. People are suffering. I will admit that there's a lot of growth in building, but for the common person, things are tight.

It must be noted that under the Kufuor Administration, the rate of exchange was 1,000 cedis per dollar. On July 1, 2007, after six and a half years in office, Kufuor changed the value of the cedi so that 1,000 of the previous cedis was now worth one. I was visiting Ghana the day when the currency value changed. The parity with the dollar was not the result of sound economic policies, but because of the Kufuor Administration's re-definition of a cedi. It is true, however, that the cedi was declining under the NDC administration, and that it had declined to the 4:1 ratio.

I asked if the respondent aspired to become a citizen of Ghana, which would be necessary in order to vote in the adopted homeland. The respondent expressed no disappointment because of the inability to vote. When talking about other Black Americans who might be frustrated in Ghana, the reply was, "For some, Ghana hasn't been all they wanted, but it is better than their past experiences before coming here."

I spoke with another expatriate who had positive things to say about the same controversial Black American politician. This respondent had worked on that politician's campaigns, and said, "He did quite a bit for his city, especially for the underclass." In Ghana this respondent is not involved in politics. The respondent was a Democrat back in the U.S., but in Ghana the respondent said, "I don't see [the parties] doing anything for the people. Colonialism is still very much intact here. The White man is still pulling the strings." Nevertheless, the respondent positively compared Rawlings to the NDC administration that was in power in Ghana at the time of the interview. The respondent said, "When Rawlings was president, he was a positive force. He would never tolerate the corruption that goes on in Ghana now." I asked if, in light of these positive feelings about Rawlings, is there a preference of Rawlings's party over the opposition NPP. The respondent said, "I don't lean toward any party here." The respondent described NPP former President Kufuor as "window dressing" for the colonial power. About one of Kufuor's moves, which was naming a major highway after George W. Bush, the respondent said, "I wanna throw up. How could you? I was extremely upset. Naming it after that fool." As for Kufuor's NDC successor, John Atta Mills, the respondent said, "I think he would've done more, but he was not well at the time. I was disappointed when he didn't sack people caught up in corruption at the harbor." Here the respondent was referring to Ghana's major commercial port, in the city of Tema, just outside of Accra. In 2013 it was reported that, due to corruption and smuggling, Ghana was losing U.S. $150 million per month![13] President Mills was not implicated in the corruption, and was reportedly extremely upset by it; he angrily confronted officials at the port, along with their security staff.[14]

I interviewed a third expatriate who also had positive things to say about that controversial Black American local politician. This respondent said, "I campaigned for him; he took care of his [constituency]." When I asked about this respondent's partisanship in the U.S., the respondent said, "Democrat, definitely!" When I enquired about the respondent's partisan leanings in Ghana, the response was, "I've adopted my [Ghanaian] spouse's persuasion: NPP." The respondent had the following to say about Ghana under Rawlings:

> When Rawlings was in power, there was a culture of silence. You couldn't say political things at the bar. I remember back in the 1980s when [dissident] Wereko-Brobby had an underground [radio] station. Nobody could find him.

During the PNDC days Charles Wereko-Brobby ran a "pirate" radio station called "Radio Eye." He played a leading role in gaining the right for private citizens to own radio stations in Ghana.[15]

The above respondent's support for the NPP was not solely based upon opposition to Rawlings, who had been out of office for over fifteen years at the time of the interview. The respondent also spoke positively about the NPP. The following was how the respondent felt about the NPP:

> The NPP, they're the people who can run the country best. . . . And Jerry Rawlings gave businesspeople a hard way to go before he started making money himself.

Here the respondent acknowledges Rawlings's abrupt transition from socialist populism to neoliberal economics. The respondent blames the transition on Rawlings's desire to make money, not upon the realization that industrialized capitalist nations had far more to offer Ghana than the East-bloc nations had, a realization that Nkrumah never arrived at. As an NPP supporter, the respondent attributes Rawlings's transition to personal greed rather than a desire to improve the macro-economy of the nation that he was leading. Here Rawlings is cast as the prototypical kleptocratic ruler, whose main goal for heading a state is to enrich himself.

One might assume that with such well-developed political leanings, the respondent would wish to have the opportunity to vote in Ghanaian elections. This respondent said that, "I have an indefinite stay visa, so why should I become a citizen? I don't care about being able to vote." I asked if the respondent is involved in any activism to persuade the Ghanaian government to grant Black Americans a right of abode, where they will have more rights than ordinary aliens. The respondent spurned involvement in such an issue, saying, "Why do we feel we have a right?

This is somebody else's country." The respondent once was involved in the effort to gain a right of abode, but is no longer involved in that struggle. The respondent expressed strong feelings on this issue:

> Once I got my indefinite stay, I didn't get involved anymore. I don't believe in giving people the right to live here just because they're Black. I got my indefinite stay because of the years I've lived here and have been married to my spouse. . . . I don't have any animosity toward the U.S. I find myself thinking of myself as a pan-African, but not for any political reasons. We shouldn't get into Ghanaian politics. I don't care about not being able to vote. . . . I'm a "[B]lack American," not an "African American." I feel we belong in the U.S.A. Why give that to White Americans? We all know that our roots are here, but we'll never be accepted as true Africans.

The respondent did acknowledge that Black Americans do face job discrimination, saying, "I see times when Black Americans were denied jobs because they weren't Ghanaians." I asked if the respondent thought that a White man would be discriminated against for the same reasons. The respondent said, "I don't think so." This led me to ask how Black Americans are treated in Ghana in general. The respondent said, "Fine, as long as we stay in our own lane," which the respondent said meant staying out of the local political arena. Another respondent expressed a similar sentiment, saying "If you wanna survive here, you'd better be apolitical. If you wanna survive as an African American, you must be apolitical; you *don't* want to be political." One of the AAPRP-affiliated respondents was even more adamant about the need to stay out of Ghanaian politics:

> When we came here, we were told not to get involved in politics. There is a danger in taking sides. It can be a problem for you. So I don't get involved."

The latter statement is quite notable, for the respondent was very much "involved" back in the United States. This involvement included protests against police brutality and against exploitative neighborhood storeowners. This activism was jettisoned after moving to Ghana.

The remarks of these respondents elucidate the difference between contemporary Ghana and Ghana during the Nkrumah era. During the

First Republic, Nkrumah placed several high profile African Americans in government positions, but such is the not the case in the Fourth Republic. The National Democratic Congress, the inaugural party of the Fourth Republic, presented itself as a successor to Nkrumah's legacy. Where they differ is that they did not open up their government to foreigners of African descent. As foreigners, African Americans are also barred from most government employment,[16] but they would not face such discrimination if dual citizenship had not been denied by parliament when it was under NDC and NPP control. Though Rawlings expressed his verbal support for dual citizenship, it was during his administration, and with his party in control of parliament, that the 2000 citizenship act was passed. That Act denies citizenship even to Ghanaian-born children whose parents are not Ghanaians.[17]

Another respondent also acknowledged that political affiliation in Ghana was influenced by associates in that country. Though this person was a Democrat back in the U.S., in Ghana the respondent states that, "As for me, personally, I would go NPP. Maybe it's because I was influenced by people in Kumasi. I'm kinda neutral, but I'm pulling for Akufo-Addo." This respondent was actively involved in Obama's presidential campaign in 2012, but sees no contradiction between that and having NPP leanings in Ghana. The respondent mentions that associating with Kumasi residents has influenced party preference in Ghana. Kumasi is the capital of the Ashanti Region, an NPP stronghold.

One of the respondents with whom I spoke supported dual citizenship, but that expatriate "do[es] not get involved in politics here." This respondent spoke of the difficulties of living in Ghana as a non-citizen, saying, "I have to go [to immigration] every year and pay $1,000." Though the respondent does not get involved in Ghanaian politics, the respondent did get involved back in the U.S. The respondent supported Jesse Jackson's presidential bids in the 1980s and voted for Barack Obama two decades later. The respondent said, "I was into helping Obama get elected the first time, but I didn't vote in 2012." As for partisanship back in the U.S., the respondent said, "When I was in the U.S., I voted in a lot of the elections. I've been both a Democrat and a Republican, but I wasn't taking it serious at that time."

Another respondent spoke of his support for Obama in 2008, but expressed some regret about it. This respondent said, "I was a Democrat, I guess, and I voted for Obama, but I regret that. I should have voted for Cynthia McKinney." Cynthia McKinney is a former Democratic member of Congress who ran for President in 2008 under the banner of the "Green Party," and on a platform far to the left of the Democratic Party.[18] I asked if the respondent has a party preference in Ghana. That question was met with an emphatic, "NO!" The respondent said, "A complete revolution should happen to this whole deal. Nothing is going to change unless we change it. With books and literature I try to enlighten people."

The above interviewee could be described as being on the political fringes, and is comfortable with neither of the two major parties in the U.S. nor of the two in Ghana. I interviewed another such person, one who was involved in civil rights demonstrations in the U.S. in the 1990s. The respondent registered as a Republican, but said, "There's no Republican I ever supported." The respondent voted for Bill Clinton in the general elections in the 1990s, and in 2008 changed party registration to Democratic in order to vote for Barack Obama in the primary election. In Ghana this respondent has lobbied to legalize marijuana, but as for parties in Ghana, the respondent said, "I don't support a political party. . . . We should never be in the pocket of a political party."

That response was similar to one given by another respondent who had no affiliation with either party back in the United States. When I asked about political involvement back in the U.S., the following was the response:

> NO! We call it 'politricks.' We won't progress as long as we think we're a part of something. I don't know how long we have to play this game that we're included in the U.S. I fought for my country in Vietnam, but the only way I can be accepted is through my death, not by politics nor by religion. That's why I came to Ghana.

When asked if the political situation seems different in Ghana, the respondent said, "I'm more of a doer than a talker. Two parties are two snakes. It's a game."

Another respondent had no regrets for having supported Obama in the 2008 election. That was the respondent's only political involvement in the United States. As for Ghana, the respondent has had some involvement in the effort to provide dual citizenship for expatriates, but that was the extent of involvement in Ghanaian politics. When asked which party the respondent would support if given the franchise in Ghana, the respondent had the following to say:

> A friend explained to me that NPP leaned more in the direction of economical growth and that NDC was famous for taking loans to complete big projects without any clear-cut plan to repay the loan. So based on that, I lean more toward NPP.

One respondent was very heavily involved in Democratic Party politics in the U.S., both on the local level and on the congressional level. The respondent had been a campaign volunteer on numerous occasions, and had even worked in Washington and developed an alliance with a Democratic U.S. senator. This respondent accepted a politically appointed government job, which led to deeper involvement in U.S. politics. Upon moving to Ghana, the respondent became involved in women's issues and in training some governmental employees. I asked if this denoted a preference with one of the two parties in Ghana. To that I received the following response:

> No! My question to those who want me to get involved in politics is "Who are you with? What are their values?" I have no affiliation at all. In the US, people I met in politics were good people, not just on their jobs. There are few such politicians here. People here do politics for political profit. That's not what politics is to me. In the US they sacrifice their money for politics. Those are the politicians there. Not so here."

Another respondent who was politically active in local Democratic politics, including in mayoral campaigns, did express some support for politicians of the NDC and for Nkrumah. The respondent said the following about Nkrumah:

> If I could, I would try to get dual citizenship. Right now, we pay 300 cedis per year. They don't seem to welcome us and our expertise, unlike the days of Nkrumah. When we do try to give advice, they say, "You too new."

Three hundred U.S. dollars is the fee charged to aliens who work for registered "Non-governmental organizations." Others must pay US $1,000. The above respondent is the same person who described Rawlings as a "positive force," and who regretted NDC President John Atta Mills faced health problems when he was in office. The respondent was less laudatory about Mills's vice president and successor, saying, "Mahama sounded good to me, but I'm not impressed with what I see."

I had assumed that, from the above statements, the respondent was a Nkrumahist, and would thus be supportive of the NDC, but I was incorrect in that assumption. President Mills was regarded as a Nkrumahist, due to his having been affiliated with the Winneba Ideological Institute during the Nkrumah years. The Winneba Ideological Institute was a Nkrumahist institution.[19] Mills's prior affiliation with the Winneba Institute led many Ghanaians to believe that he was a Nkrumahist. When Rawlings picked Mills as his vice president, back in 1996, he was demonstrating that the NDC was the home for disciples of Ghana's first president. Indeed many Nkrumahists have flocked to the NDC during the Fourth Republic, but some have avoided supporting the party, and do not see the NDC as a successor to Nkrumah's Convention People's Party.[20] The above respondent is one who reveres Nkrumah but is not a supporter of the NDC. The respondent said, "I don't lean toward any party here. Just like Republicans and Democrats in the U.S., when the rubber hits the road, it's the same."

I spoke with one respondent who was involved with the campaign of a Democratic mayoral candidate back in the United States. This respondent was somewhat defensive of the then-current NDC President John Mahama. The interview was conducted in the immediate aftermath of a government program of rationing of electric power, which resulted in scheduled periodic blackouts, which Ghanaians called "*dum sɔ*," meaning "off-on." The opposition NPP was using the blackouts as a campaign issue to oust Mahama from power.[21] When I asked if Mahama deserved the blame, the respondent gave the following answer:

> Hell no! We should teach structure [to people who blame Mahama]. Tell them that the IMF stipulations are to blame. The NPP uses *dum sɔ* as a slogan against Mahama. What they have failed to say is that the turbines came from the British, and the [IMF] stipulation is that they have to buy them from the British.

I thought that the above statement might have indicated a preference for the NDC. The respondent denied that such was the case, and said that "Both parties are the same, just like in the U.S."

Figure 2. Steven Taylor and John Atta Mills, August 18, 2007, in Worcester Massachusetts (author's collection).

## Similarities Between the Partisan Structures of Ghana and the United States

What I discovered was that even those respondents who were politically active in the U.S. put that activism behind them when they arrived in Ghana. There were some exceptions. One was the previously mentioned respondent who was involved in women's issues, equal pay, and who opposed the abandonment of English as the official language. As a college student, that respondent had a political column in the campus newspaper, wrote on issues pertaining to foreign policy, and also became involved in women's issues, even organizing an "Equal Pay Day," in the city in which the college was located. This interviewee was also on a Title 9 advisory committee, about gender equity in educational programs, and was involved in the Black student organization at the college. Many Ghanaians share this expatriate's concern that replacing English will be discriminatory against students who are linguistic minorities in the regions where they reside. Students from linguistic minority groups are often far more familiar with written English than with the written language that will be adopted in the schools they attend. The proposed policy will be especially harmful to non-Akans, who are more likely than Akans to reside in areas where they are linguistic minorities. Though the NDC has most of its strength among the non-Akans, it was Mahama's Minister of Education who proposed this change.[22] Perhaps this is why the respondent does not have a preference for that party. The respondent said, "It's interesting. Most people I encounter in Accra are NPP, but outside of Accra it's NDC. There are not a lot of things I see that I like about the NDC, but I'm still observing."

The respondent is correct in stating that the NPP has strength in the urban areas, while the NDC is stronger in the rural areas. This rural-urban partisan divide has existed from the first days of the Fourth Republic.[23] Many urban dwellers questioned Rawlings's qualifications for the office of the presidency. They pointed to his limited academic preparation (Rawlings's only academic credential is a high school diploma)[24] and his lack of sophistication[25] (he once beat up his own vice president during a cabinet meeting).[26] Rural voters were less disturbed by such factors, and they saw the NDC as the party who helped develop their area by delivering such essential amenities as electricity and water.[27]

Most of the respondents had been Democrats back in the U.S., or were independents who leaned toward the Democratic Party. This I expected, as the respondents were African Americans, and African Americans exhibit strong loyalty toward the Democratic Party, more than any other demographic group in the U.S. shows to any of the political parties in that country. This nearly undivided loyalty among African Americans began in 1964, when the two parties took very different positions on the issue that was of deepest concern to African Americans, and that was the issue of civil rights. African Americans' move to the Democratic Party dates back to the Great Depression. In 1936, for the first time in U.S. history, a vast majority of Black voters supported the Democratic presidential candidate, the incumbent Franklin Delano Roosevelt.[28] Though Roosevelt was no vocal supporter of civil rights, the economic policies of his "New Deal" endeared him to African Americans, many of whom were severely impoverished during the Great Depression. The Depression marked a political realignment that saw Black voters put an end to their 70-year-old affiliation with the Republican Party and move to the Democratic Party. Despite this massive shift in party allegiance, the Republican Party did maintain some Black support, and this was seen in the election of 1956. That year, incumbent Republican President Dwight David Eisenhower received 39 percent of the Black vote, the highest level of any Republican since 1932.[29] In 1960 Eisenhower's vice president, Richard M. Nixon, received 32 percent of the Black vote, which was a very respectable showing for a Republican. But in the next presidential election—1964—the Republican nominee Senator Barry Goldwater received only 6 percent of the Black vote, whereas President Lyndon B. Johnson, the Democratic candidate, received 94 percent.[30] That election marked another turning point. It was the first time that the Republican Party abandoned even a pretense of commitment to civil rights. Four months before that election, President Johnson had signed a landmark civil rights bill, whose purpose was to guarantee equal access to public accommodations, employment, and voting. Goldwater was one of a small number of members of Congress to oppose the bill. This policy shift among the parties has resulted in the Democratic Party losing the support of the South, but gaining the unflinching loyalty of Black voters. Subsequent elections demonstrate that 1964 was no aberration. Since then the Democratic Party has received well over 80 percent of the Black vote, sometimes topping 90 percent. The Republican Party's performance among African Americans has often been down in the single digits.[31]

My initial assumption was that African-Americans' disdain for the Republican Party in the U.S. would lead to their rejection of that party's Ghanaian counterpart, the New Patriotic Party. The NPP is modeled after the U.S. Republican Party, even using the same mascot (the elephant) and carrying the colors red, white, and blue, despite the fact that Ghana's flag is red, black, green, and gold. I had hypothesized that the respondents would, as a whole, reject the Ghanaian party that was a local version of the Republican Party, and would embrace the party that claims to be the heir of two presidents—Nkrumah and Rawlings—who invited Black Americans to Ghana. The findings from my ethnographic data do not corroborate my initial hypothesis. Among the African-American respondents there was no groundswell of support for the National Democratic Congress. This differs from the days of the First Republic. The secondary materials that I have studied from that earlier era demonstrate that African Americans residing in Ghana back then were, almost to a person, loyal to Kwame Nkrumah and his Convention People's Party. The major party who sells itself as a successor to Nkrumah does not command the same level of support among Black Americans that Nkrumah enjoyed.

During the Fourth Republic, Ghana has offered political choices somewhat similar to those in the United States. Though the 1992 election that ushered in the Fourth Republic was disputed, the second election, that of 1996 was not. Rawlings was reelected, and his NDC retained control of parliament, but they faced a visible and growing opposition party that was represented in parliament. After the 1996 elections the NDC held 133 seats in Ghana's 200-member parliament, while the NPP held 60 seats.[32] In other words, the NDC and the NPP had a duopoly that controlled 97 percent of the seats in parliament. Duopolies also reign in the United States, Great Britain, Canada, and many other English-speaking democracies. This is because these countries have single-member parliamentary districts and no provision for proportional representation, which would allow minor parties to receive some representation. In a multi-party system there are issues-based smaller parties that represent the interests of ideological minority groups. These parties sometimes play a major role if no party receives a majority of the parliamentary seats. In such situations, minor parties are invited to help form a coalition government, thus giving legitimacy to the smaller parties. Such situations rarely occur in a duopoly, where the smaller parties are not attractive coalition partners because they do not win enough seats in parliament. All governance is in the hands of the two major parties, which control the legislature and the presidency. This is what is seen both in Ghana and in the United States.

Anthony Downs is an economist who likened democracies to the economic free market, and explained how political parties position themselves in a duopoly. In a free market system, entrepreneurs establish their businesses in locations where they are accessible to the largest number of customers. Therefore, competing businesses are often located in close proximity to one another, in locations where they can receive the highest number of customers. This disadvantages those customers who live in isolated locations, but it does not disadvantage the business owners. Customers in remote areas have no choice but to travel to the more populous regions in order to purchase products. There is no incentive for business owners to set up establishments in remote locations. They will be far more successful by locating themselves in the heavily populated regions, where they will be patronized by customers from that lucrative region, and also by customers in remote locations who have no other choices. Such is the same with political parties in a two-party system. Downs posits that the ideological preferences of the voters are arrayed in a bell-shaped curve, with most voters at the ideological center of that curve.[33] Parties who wish to govern will position themselves toward the center in order that they will maximize the number of votes they will receive in an election. In a two-party system this results in the parties converging toward each other and demonstrating few differences. This is precisely the situation in Ghana, which is why some of the respondents stated that the parties are virtually indistinguishable from one another.

There is some merit to the argument that the NDC and NPP are similar. Though the NDC purports to be the home of the Nkrumahists, they abandoned socialism back in the days when they were the PNDC. Rawlings and his successors of both parties have embraced free market economics, and have limited the intervention of the state. A minor issue in which the two parties have converged is the naming of the previously mentioned highway. Though it was NPP President Kufuor who promised his friend Bush that the highway would be named after him, it was during the administration of NDC President Mills when the highway was named.[34] That this Nkrumahist named a major Ghanaian roadway after a right-wing U.S. president shows how much the Nkrumahist and the Danquah/Busia political traditions have converged over the decades.

On the other side of Ghana's political divide, the NPP, which models itself after center-right parties of the Western world, developed a national health insurance program. The "Ghana National Health Insurance Scheme" was established in 2003 during the NPP administration of John A. Kufuor, and its goal is universal health care.[35] The NPP has also made some movement on another one of Nkrumah's passions, and that is outreach toward descendants of the Atlantic Slave Trade. In 2007 the Kufuor Administration launched the "Joseph Project" to reach out to Diasporan Africans. The project was headed by Jake Obetsebi-Lamptey, Ghana's Minister of Tourism and Disaporan Relations. Among the goals of the Project were to encourage Diasporan Africans (Including Black Americans) to vacation in Ghana and to consider settling there. Another stated goal was to open an "African Union (AU) Diasporan Office . . . to be located in Ghana." This office would serve the purpose of "work[ing] on

Diasporan issues with AU member countries"[36] The office has been named the Diaspora Africa Forum (DAF), and an ambassador was appointed to represent Diasporans before the African Union. The DAF's ambassadorial mission was dedicated on Sunday, July 1, 2007, and a plaque was presented by President Kufuor. I was present at the start of that ceremony. One month before the opening of the mission, Jake Obetsebi-Lamptey was interviewed on National Public Radio in the United States. Obetsebi-Lamptey invoked the names of Nkrumah and Du Bois.[37] The irony is that Obetsebi-Lamptey's father, Emmanuel Obetsebi-Lamptey, was a virulent opponent of Nkrumah.[38] Also ironic is that the NDC, which presents itself as the successor to Nkrumah, allowed the Joseph Project to languish when they returned to power in 2009.

As is the case with Ghana, the U.S. has a two-party democracy in which those two parties converge on many issues. Prior to 2016, both parties were somewhat centrist, with the Democratic Party being center-left and the Republican Party being center-right. The Democratic Party is not a socialist party, nor does it profess to be. Contrary to political rhetoric on the right, the Democrats do not favor a massive redistribution of wealth and government confiscation of privately owned corporations. Nor does the Democratic Party plan to decimate the defense budget. It was under the administration of Barack Obama that the U.S. military conducted a troop surge in Afghanistan in hopes of defeating the Taliban. Bill Clinton, the last Democratic president prior to Obama, boasted of being a "New Democrat" much closer to the center than Democratic presidential aspirants of the 1980s. Clinton abandoned the Keynesian economic policies of Democratic presidents since Roosevelt, and his reductions in spending led to three consecutive balanced federal budgets, yielding surpluses. Rather than using these surpluses to increase spending on social programs, Clinton used the additional revenue to pay down the national debt.[39] In addition to this, he also passed a draconian welfare reform act, making good on his vow to "End welfare as we know it."[40] The Democratic presidents of the twenty-first century have steered their Party down a centrist path.

Prior to 2016 the Republican Party avoided the right-wing extremism of some of the parties that have won parliamentary seats in Europe. Though Ronald Reagan was seen by some as a personification of the extreme right, Reagan avoided the most hostile expressions of anger voiced by members of the far right. While he did indeed placate the far right by making William Rehnquist the Chief Justice of the Supreme Court and appointing Antonin Scalia as an Associate Justice, he also elevated to the Court two centrists who were abortion rights supporters: Sandra Day O'Connor and Anthony Kennedy. While the right-wing parties in Europe are centered around their opposition to immigration, Reagan took a far different stance. In 1986 he signed legislation granting amnesty to millions of undocumented workers who entered the U.S. illegally.[41]

Reagan even provided a semblance of moderation on issues of concern to African Americans, the segment of the population where he had his lowest level of support. In the 1960s Reagan opposed the Civil Rights Act, the Voting Rights Act, and the Fair Housing Act.[42] As president, however, he signed into law the holiday commemorating Martin Luther King, the person who did more than any other American to secure the passage of the civil rights laws that Reagan opposed. To the surprise of some, in 1982 Reagan signed into law an extension of the 1965 Voting Rights Act that he had previously opposed. These moves by Reagan were a way in which he appealed to the vote-rich political center.

Reagan, however, was careful not to alienate his racially conservative base. Designating a holiday in honor of a civil rights leader did nothing to secure the civil rights of potential victims of discrimination. Moreover, the Voting Rights Act that Reagan extended is toothless unless it is vigorously enforced by the Justice Department. That department is always under the control of the president, which at that time was Reagan himself. The strength of the Voting Rights Act depends upon the level of support the Act receives from the president. President Reagan was not as generous when it came to legislation that would have advanced civil rights without his interference. In 1988 Congress passed a civil rights act that would deny federal funds to educational institutions that have programs that practice discrimination. When the bill came to President Reagan's desk, he promptly vetoed it. That was the first time a president had vetoed a civil rights act in more than a century. At that time, the Democrats held the majority of both houses of Congress. Using their majority, along with the support of a minority of Republicans, Congress was able to override the veto. President Reagan also used his veto in legislation pertaining to civil rights abroad. During the international movement to end apartheid in South Africa, the U.S. Congress passed sanctions against the White minority regime in South Africa. President Reagan vetoed the sanctions bill. As with the Civil Rights bill of 1988, Reagan faced the near-unanimous opposition of congressional Democrats and a minority of Republicans, and the veto was overridden. Prior to that veto, the Reagan Administration violated the United Nations arms embargo on South Africa, vetoed a U.N. Security Council resolution that would have imposed sanctions on the apartheid regime, and even approved a $1.1 billion loan to South Africa from the International Monetary Fund. The excuse for these friendly gestures toward the racist government was that this was "constructive engagement" that would allow the U.S. to have more influence to make changes in South Africa.[43]

Reagan's vice president and successor, George H. W. Bush, also had a long history of opposing civil rights legislation. In 1964, when he was running for the U.S. Senate as the Republican nominee from Texas, Bush strongly opposed the Civil Rights Act, as did his party's presidential nominee, Barry Goldwater. The Civil Rights Act faced an even more formidable obstacle: the U.S. Supreme Court. By the time that Bush became president, the Supreme Court had a Republican majority, and was led by William Rehnquist, one of the most conservative Supreme Court justices of the twentieth century. In the late 1980s and early 1990s the Rehnquist court issued a series of decisions that eviscerated the fair employment portion (Title VII) of the 1964 Civil Rights Act. In 1989, in the *Wards Cove Packing Company vs. Atonio* Decision, the Court ruled in favor of a company that did not provide non-White manual laborers the opportunity to apply for supervisory positions.[44] In another 1989 case, *Patterson vs. McLean Credit Union*, the Court ruled that Title VII of the Civil Rights Act does not forbid racial harassment and discrimination on the job, but only covers the contractual (hiring) phase.[45] In 1990 the Democratic majority of Congress passed a Civil Rights Act that clarified the equal employment provisions of the 1964 act, and which would proscribe the actions at issue in the *Patterson vs. McLean* and *Wards Cove* cases. President George H. W. Bush vetoed that Civil Rights Act, stating that it would lead to racial quotas. The Democratic leadership of Congress fell short in their efforts to gain enough Republican support to override the veto. In 1991 the Supreme Court issued another decision that helped decimate Title VII. In the *E.E.O.C. vs. Arabian American Oil Company* case, the Court ruled that Title VII did not apply to U.S. corporations operating abroad.[46] Later that year Congress passed a bill very similar to the bill passed one year earlier, and President Bush threatened to veto that legislation also. However, he was in the midst of a fight to appoint a very conservative federal judge to the U.S. Supreme Court, one who was replacing liberal icon Thurgood

Marshall. In the midst of those negotiations, Bush signed the bill, and the Senate allowed the nominee to sit on the Supreme Court. That member of the Supreme Court, along with the rest of the Republican majority on the Court, has been consistent in supporting Court decisions that are opposed by supporters of civil rights, while the Democratic minority on the court has been just as consistent in supporting civil rights.

Despite the fact that there have been some cosmetic attempts at moderation, the Republican Party has taken a distinct stand in opposition to civil rights, while the Democratic Party has supported civil rights. This trend began in the 1960s, and it has become more pronounced ever since. If one were to look at the plethora of issues that make up the U.S. political landscape, the two major parties appear to converge. However, on the issue most salient to African Americans—civil rights and anti-discrimination—the parties do not converge. Downsian theory of unimodality applies when one looks at the entire panorama of political issues, but when certain single issues are isolated, the public is often not unimodal. Civil rights and anti-discrimination is an issue that brings about bimodality among the U.S. public. While the general public has moved away from the support that it gave to civil rights back in the 1960s, African Americans remain staunch supporters of civil rights and equal opportunities for racial minorities. Meanwhile Black Americans have become the electoral base of the Democratic Party. This has moved the Party to the left on civil rights, away from the political center on that issue. When it comes to civil rights, there is now a bimodal distribution, with a peak on the left representing African Americans and a much taller peak on the right of the scale, which represents White Americans. The African-American base of the Democratic Party refuses to allow the party to move rightward on civil rights, which has caused the Party to lose some presidential elections. It has also resulted in the parties looking very different from each other on this single issue. For voters who see this as the most salient issue, the two parties do appear to be very different, which explains African-American loyalty to the Democratic Party.

The current cadre of elected officials in the United States reflects the bimodality of the general public on civil rights issues, and demonstrates strong partisan differences. These differences, however, did not always exist. In the 1960s there were Democrats who bucked their Party's leadership and opposed civil rights measures. These were mainly Southern Democrats. When the Civil Rights Act was passed in 1964, All but one of the U.S. senators from the former Confederate states voted "nay." Twenty one of those senators were Democrats, and the only Southern Democrat to support the bill was Ralph Yarbrough of Texas, who would be challenged by George H. W. Bush for his pro-civil rights vote. Outside of the South, all 46 Democratic senators supported the bill, and 27 of the 32 Republicans supported the bill.[47] This demonstrated a bipartisan support for Civil Rights. By the 1990s that bipartisanship over civil rights had disappeared, both among the proponents and the opponents. When Congress passed the 1990 Civil Rights Act (which Bush vetoed), all 55 Democrats in the U.S. Senate voted for the Act, including the 15 from the South. All 34 opponents of the bill were Republicans, while only 11 Republicans supported the bill. It must be noted that not one of those 11 is still in the Senate. Back in 1964 there was bipartisan opposition of and bipartisan support for civil rights. The Democratic opposition came from the Southern Democrats, but by 1990 all Southern Democratic senators were in support of Civil Rights. There was also bi-partisan support in 1964, with 84 percent of the non-Southern Republican senators supporting the Act. By 1990 the situation was far different. One hundred percent of Democrats in the U.S. Senate—Southern and non-Southern—voted for the civil rights act that year, while 76 percent of the Republicans opposed it.[48] Of that 24 percent of Republicans who supported the Civil Rights Act of 1990, not one remains in the U.S. Senate, greatly diminishing the prospects for future bipartisan support for civil rights legislation. The Southern Democratic opponents of Civil Rights have left the political scene. Persons such as Herman Talmadge and Richard Russell of Georgia, Russell Long of Louisiana, and George Smathers of Florida have no current duplicates in the U.S. Senate. Similarly, the liberal Republican civil rights proponents have gone. There are no more liberal Republicans such as Jacob Javits of New York, Clifford Case of New Jersey, Hugh Scott of Pennsylvania, or George Aiken of Vermont. The Republican Party is united in its opposition to civil rights legislation, while the Democratic Party is united in its support. Though the two parties may converge on many other issues, they remain poles apart on civil rights, and as a result the African-American segment of the electorate is solidly supportive of the Democratic Party.

Among African Americans residing in Ghana, there are no such salient issues that divide the parties. Therefore, there is no generally preferred party among the expatriates, as there had been in the early 1960s. What separates the two major parties in Ghana is region and ethnicity.

The NPP is the preferred party among the Akans, while the NDC is preferred among the ethnic groups based in the north and among the Ewes in the east. Since African Americans belong to none of these ethnic groups, there is no party that can claim their allegiance as a whole.

There is a small minority of the African-American community that identifies itself as socialist, and therefore pays more attention to class issues than to racial issues. This left wing of the African-American electorate is not impressed by the Democratic Party's support of civil rights. While supportive of civil rights, as socialists they are equally concerned with issues such as poverty and full employment and militarization. On these issues the parties in Ghana and the U.S. tend to converge, which makes socialists reluctant to support none of the major parties in either country. The AAPRP is an avowedly socialist organization, and its members in Ghana expressed disappointment with the major parties in the U.S. and in Ghana.

I spoke to a respondent who stated that the extent of involvement in U.S. politics was "Attending one or two meetings with a left-wing party." The respondent shunned political involvement in the U.S. because "the U.S. was an empire under the Democrats or the Republicans. . . . The multinational corporations control things." The respondent is not involved in Ghanaian politics either, but stated that if given the franchise, "I'd probably be involved with a minor party."

Another respondent who identified with the political left in the U.S. worked as a lobbyist before leaving the U.S. In Ghana this respondent is supportive of both major parties. The respondent had the following to say about the parties in Ghana as they relate to the concerns of African Americans:

> The right of abode has been discussed with the government. Nkrumah, Rawlings and Kufuor made some moves in that direction. Kufuor made moves and stood firmly at the African Union. Even his minister of Tourism, Jake (Lamptey) made it a priority, but it has dwindled under the NDC. [Nevertheless], I have a strong relationship with both parties.

Another respondent expressed support for an insurgent Democrat who once sought his party's presidential nomination, but in this case the insurgent was civil rights leader Jesse Jackson. The respondent had the following to say about political activities in the U.S.:

I didn't even vote in the U.S. I'm not even registered. I registered in 1988 when Jesse ran. I was a Democrat. Jesse had everybody's blood stirring. That's the last time I had an appreciation for "politricks." It's just like here.

When asked about his partisan preference in Ghana, the above respondent expressed praise for Jerry Rawlings:

There was a welcome there. What Nkrumah started, another leader [later continued]. JJ is what brought me here. JJ said, "If Jews can come back to Israel, Blacks can come to Ghana. But JJ's successor Kufuor dissed it."

When I asked if the respondent had any party affiliation in a post-Rawlings Ghana, the respondent said the following:

NO! Politics wasn't my concern. Peace of mind was my concern. If I were involved in politics, I wouldn't know which party to choose. To tell you the truth, I like JJ. I want him to come back to office now. He brought discipline. The more democratized a country is, the more they forget themselves. Democracy is not for Africa. Look at the socio-cultural entities—Chieftaincy—should you break that down? During JJ's time, there were curfews, discipline, and no armed robbers. JJ would knock 'em all out.

One respondent whom I interviewed self-classified as an "independent," and expressed support for politicians who had held elected and appointed positions from both the Republican and Democratic Parties. This respondent praised politicians from the far-left to the center-right of the U.S. political spectrum. The respondent was supportive of Cynthia McKinney (Green Party), Bernie Sanders (Independent socialist), Democrats Elizabeth Warren, John Lewis, and Elijah Cummins, Republican Colin Powell, and Republican-turned-Libertarian William Weld. In Ghana the respondent leans toward the NPP and has been somewhat active supporting a bill to provide voting rights to Ghanaians living abroad. The respondent believes that most African-American repatriates are sympathetic to the NDC, and this is probably because the NDC has sponsored legislation designed to give citizenship rights to repatriates. However, this respondent is also an entrepreneur, and stated that back in the U.S. most Ghanaians who helped support the establishment of the respondent's non-governmental organization (NGO) were NPP partisans. The respondent disagrees with the notion that the NPP is an extension of the U.S. Republican Party, stating that, "the NPP is also very aggressive with a Pan African Agenda." The respondent cites the "Joseph Project" as an example. The respondent then corrected the earlier statement about the affinity toward the NDC among repatriates, and said, "Repatriates I know are mostly non-partisan. We try to network whoever is in power."

I had the good fortune of interviewing one of the persons who repatriated to Ghana during the Nkrumah years, one of the "Politicals." This respondent was married to a politically active Ghanaian, and was politically active when living in the U.S., exclusively with the Democratic Party. Though the respondent could not vote in Ghanaian elections, during the First Republic the respondent supported Nkrumah. About the 1960 election, the respondent said, "Nkrumah over Danquah. Definitely!" The respondent has remained in Ghana, and during the Fourth Republic has been an NDC supporter and favored both Rawlings and Mills. However, by 2016, the respondent was not enthusiastic about the incumbent NDC president. An election was scheduled to be held in eight months, but the respondent was not certain as to whom to support, saying "If I were a Ghanaian, I don't know whom I would vote for."

Anthony Downs's theory is very general, and he does not discuss single-issue voting, but alludes to the wide array of issues that dominate a country's political landscape. In this section of this book, I examine one issue, the issue most important to my respondents. On this particular issue—civil rights—the U.S. public is not unimodal. On the right side of the spectrum are those very much opposed to any civil rights measure, while on the left side are those who are supportive. Downs said that what keeps parties from an ideological convergence is from the refusal of extremist voters to support either party if both become similar.[49] The most vehement opponents of civil rights are a key part of the GOP's constituency, while the strongest proponents are a part of the Democratic Party's core constituency. Despite the parties' similarity on other issues, their differences over civil rights have led to the monopartisanship of African Americans. In Ghana, however, civil rights is not an issue, and it certainly is not one in which the parties diverge. For this reason, the mono-partisanship of African Americans in the U.S. is not replicated in Ghana. Therefore, unlike during the days when the African-American community was led by the "Politicals," today's expatriates are not wed to one particular political party.

## Focus on Meeting Basic Needs of the Populace

There is no daylight between Ghana's two major parties on the issue that is of utmost concern to many in the expatriate community: giving descendants of the slave trade the rights accorded to citizens of Ghana. This has not been a priority of the Ghanaian government, not even when it was controlled by the NDC, the party that first proposed granting citizenship to Black expatriates from the western hemisphere. The failure to prioritize a pan-African measure such as this can be explained by Ronald Inglehart, whose research concerning Europe and the U.S. is also applicable to West Africa. Inglehart uses a cohort analysis and finds that cohorts who experienced scarcities in essential goods will prioritize economic security. Similarly, those cohorts who endured wars will prioritize physical security.[50] This analysis is based upon the hierarchy explained by Abraham Maslow. According to Maslow, if the most basic physiological needs are not met, individuals have little concern for higher order needs. If, however, the most basic needs are met, then the focus is on safety and security, which is the next to lowest level. These two lowest levels are basic needs. Beyond that are psychological needs, and at the highest level are self-fulfillment needs.[51] Pan-Africanist goals are on the level of self-fulfillment needs, but Ghana is a society where many citizens are struggling to meet their physiological needs. Therefore, public officials accord low priority to achieving unity between Ghanaians and their long-lost Diasporic relatives from across the Ocean. In a democratic setting, as Ghana is today, politicians cannot expect to remain in office if they fail to continually address the issues that the electorate prioritizes. It is only in an authoritarian setting, in which officials do not face free and fair elections, where they have the luxury of focusing on issues that are of little concern to the electorate.

A similar existed situation existed during the time when many African Americans faced the same economic deprivations that Ghanaians face today: the Great Depression. In the early 1930s, African Americans (and many other Americans) faced starvation, homelessness, and joblessness at rates never seen before. The Great Depression brought many Americans down to the lowest level of the Maslowian hierarchy: physiological needs. At the start of the Depression, a vast majority of African Americans identified with the Republican Party, as they had for seven decades. In 1933, Democrat Franklin Roosevelt became president and began implementing his "New Deal" programs that provided jobs and relief to those who were suffering, a disproportionate number of whom were Black. When Roosevelt ran for reelection in 1936, he had the overwhelming support of African Americans, and began a marriage between Blacks and the Democratic Party, a marriage that continues to this day. During the 1930s, however, the Democratic Party was not the champion of civil rights that it would become in the 1960s. Roosevelt himself was no vocal supporter of civil rights, and made no effort to eliminate segregation, not even in government programs and facilities. However, Black voters saw him as addressing their most pressing concern at that time: meeting their basic needs for sustenance. A glaring example was the National Housing Act of 1937, which provided for the construction of housing for low-income citizens. In the underwriting manual developed by the Federal Housing Administration (which oversaw the public housing developments throughout the country), administrators are instructed to ascertain that the developments would be racially segregated.[52] For African Americans in search of affordable housing, segregated housing was preferable to none at all. The Depression was a brief era when dismantling Jim Crow was not the top priority of African Americans. This is why they voted for Roosevelt, despite his lack of support for civil rights.

The Depression was followed by World War II, when the primary concern of Americans, regardless of race, was safety and security, the second-to-lowest level of Maslow's hierarchy. Again President Roosevelt was seen as addressing these needs, and he maintained his support among African Americans. When the War ended (after Roosevelt had died), African-American leaders stepped up their efforts to end Jim Crow. For many, their lower-level needs (physiological needs and safety and security) were taken care of, so they made efforts to meet their higher-level needs. This is vastly different from Ghana, where the economy has not developed to the degree whereby the electorate will express concern about higher-level needs. Pan-African solidarity falls among the higher-level needs that are not yet prioritized in Ghana.

# 4

# Entrepreneurs and Educators

## Challenges of Non-Citizenship

The avoidance of political activity of the current generation of expatriates in Ghana displays a fundamental difference between them and the first generation, whose involvement in politics and government gained them the moniker "the Politicals." A similarity between the two generations is that they both responded to invitations by Ghanaian presidents. The Politicals came in response to Kwame Nkrumah's call to come and help build the newly independent country. This invitation went out to those who would help run the new government, and also to those who supported his political vision. Nkrumah, the former Presbyterian minister, was known to have coined his own variant of Matthew 6:33, which says, "But seek ye first the kingdom of God, and his righteousness; and all these things shall be added unto you." Nkrumah made a slight change in the wording by stating, "Seek ye first the political kingdom, and all things shall be added unto you."[1] Nkrumah welcomed exiles from the United States and other countries to help him in that "search" for the "political kingdom."

When Jerry Rawlings renewed Nkrumah's invitation three decades later, he was not looking for any assistance in the political development of Ghana. Rawlings's primary goal was the economic development of Ghana. He did not wish to extend political control beyond his authoritarian PNDC, but he knew that economic growth could not occur without the assistance of foreign investors. His message to African Americans was that they too were welcome in helping to build the economy of his country. Consequently, many of those African Americans who repatriated during the Rawlings and post-Rawlings era went as entrepreneurs, not as political exiles. However, one must not walk away with the impression that there is no altruistic spirit among the more recent expatriates, for many have also come as educators at all levels of schooling. Some of those who came as business entrepreneurs have also made educational contributions either by teaching, academic advising, or helping to pay for the educational expenses of Ghanaian children.

Seven of the persons whom I interviewed moved to Ghana either as entrepreneurs or as the wives of Ghanaians living in the U.S., and who returned to Ghana to establish businesses. Three of these entrepreneurial expatriates were also educators, either through teaching or through holding administrative positions at the University of Ghana. In addition to those three, another eight interviewees came exclusively as educators, at all levels, from the elementary level to the university level.

The businesses owned by the respondents varied in size and in function. Some of the owners expressed frustration at the Ghana Investment Act of 1994, which places very stringent restrictions on non-Ghanaians, preventing them from owning property, from establishing small businesses without having a Ghanaian partner, and from remaining in the country without paying a sizable annual fee (US $1,000). In order for a foreigner to own a business with a Ghanaian partner, that foreigner must put up a minimum of $10,000 U.S. in equity with a Ghanaian partner. Without a Ghanaian partner the minimum is $50,000. If the business is a "trading enterprise involved in only the purchasing and selling of goods," the minimum equity rises to $300,000 and must employ at least ten Ghanaian citizens.[2] In addition, foreigners are forbidden from owning the following types of businesses:[3]

1. Businesses where sale is conducted through hawking or in a kiosk
2. A taxicab enterprise unless the proprietor provides ten *new* vehicles
3. Gambling enterprises
4. Beauty salons and barber shops.

These restrictions place severe limitations on entrepreneurial expatriates, and for that reason some have involved themselves in the struggle for dual citizenship, or, at the very least, a "Right of Abode," whereby they can establish enterprises in Ghana unencumbered by the regulations of the Ghana Investment Act.

One expatriate who has plans to open up businesses in Ghana had the following to say about the involvement of African Americans in lobbying the Ghanaian parliament to pass an operational "Right of Abode."

> Back when Rawlings introduced the right of abode, we sat in on meetings. It became a legislative instrument, and then it became a bill. But despite that, ask them who has obtained that right. One prominent expatriate couple, paid the money, and then they were denied. I'm not going to apply because I don't want to lose money like they did.
>
> The right of abode is part of Rawlings's legacy. It was then supported by the next government through Jake Lamptey's "Joseph Project." But what came of it, after that government came out of power? What we had as a bill, the NPP turned into a "Project," the Joseph Project.

Another interviewee also spoke of an expatriate paying the fee to receive the "Right of Abode," but having that petition denied without the fee being returned.

I was present at a meeting wherein a government official was lobbied about the right of expatriates of African descent to remain in Ghana. The meeting was held on April 23, 2016, and the official was Nii Kweisi Quartey, who was the executive secretary to then-President Mahama. This was the monthly meeting of the African Youth Improvement Foundation's Ministry of the Future. The regular attendees were expatriates from the U.S. and the Caribbean. Members complained to Mr. Quartey about the false hopes that the government had given them about the prospect of receiving dual citizenship. Quartey's response was, "You must take into account the various laws, the resolution of which is not easy." The meeting became tense later when Quartey referred to the expatriate community as "Your people." To that an expatriate said, "Your People? You're my people too." Quartey retorted by saying, "Sometimes, by the way you speak, I don't think you see me as your people." He then smiled and said, "But this is all in jest." He suggested that if they had concerns, they could, "write a petition to articulate your concerns." This suggestion did nothing to diffuse the tensions. One attendee mocked the idea of submitting petitions to the judicial system in Ghana, which still retains the trappings of English colonization. The attendee ridiculed the idea of "Go[ing] to people wearing white wigs—colonial authorities. You want our money, but you don't wanna give us our rights. It's all B.S.!" This expatriate was referring to the fact that in Ghana the judges wear white wigs and red robes, a custom they borrowed from the British colonizers.

Several persons at the meeting talked about negative experiences that expatriates have had with immigration authorities. The following was a description of an expatriate's encounter with immigration officials:

> Two years ago a Deputy Minister was here [meeting with this group] and said we could get our citizenship. We got his card, we called and got no answers. It's all rhetoric. I get in fights when I'm treated like a foreigner. I got arrested for insisting that I'm Ghanaian at immigration. So how do we get our rights back that were taken from us?

One attendee described an encounter that a female expatriate had with the Criminal Investigation Department (CID) of Ghana. When CID officers asked her what country she was a citizen of, she replied, "Heaven." The heavenly citizen was promptly arrested. The convener of the meeting reminded the attendees that, "The Ghanaian government watches us very closely. They monitor us. They want to know if you contribute." The consensus among the expatriates at the meeting was that a solution was dual citizenship. The convener of the meeting noted that dual citizenship was placed before Parliament in 1999, but it was rejected. The convener also made note of the fact that the "The Joseph Project was organized in 2007, but it never got off of the ground."

One entrepreneur who was present at the meeting complained about the inconvenience, both logistical and financial, of paying the annual $1,000 fee to remain in Ghana. However, businesspersons who are not a part of the African Youth Improvement Foundation are far more conservative and not as vociferous in the quest for a Right of Abode or dual citizenship. One entrepreneur and educator, the previously quoted person who so strongly rejected the idea of race-based citizenship for Black Americans, did acknowledge that, "It [would be] easier to have a five-year permit rather than doing it every year."

## African-American Educators in Ghana

Ghana offers opportunities for college graduates who wish to go into the teaching profession, but who may not have certification to teach in U.S. schools. For some this gives them the opportunity to receive pedagogical experience and training, which helps them launch a teaching career in Ghana, or which may provide them with invaluable experience before they return to the U.S. to gain certification and enter the teaching profession. One of the respondents came to Ghana as a volunteer teacher, but is now a full-time paid teacher. This respondent plans to return to the United States to receive a graduate degree before embarking upon a teaching career in the United States. Meanwhile there is frustration at the difficulties imposed upon expatriates who reside in Ghana. The respondent said, "I don't know why it's so difficult to get a Right of Abode."

One of the entrepreneurs, who had also worked as a teacher in Ghana, seemed to sense an unfairness in the law that required a $1,000 fee, in that teachers were not exempted. The respondent correctly stated that persons working for non-government organizations (NGOs) only have to pay $300, but that for others, "[Even] for teachers, it's $1,000." That respondent was one of nine respondents who are employed in the education sector.

Another U.S.-born educator, one whom I did not have the opportunity to interview, was the subject of an article about the educational institution that she had established for young children. In February 2017 the *Chicago Sun Times* printed an article about Patricia Wilkins, entitled "Brooklyn Native Gave up Everything. Now Serves Poor in Ghana." In 2000 Ms. Wilkins gave up a lucrative career as a fashion designer, rid herself of most of her possessions, and moved to Ghana to serve as an educational volunteer. In 2004 she opened up her own school, whose purpose is to serve impoverished children who would not otherwise have an opportunity to receive a formal education in Ghana. She now runs three schools.[4]

Another U.S.-born educator, Akosua Boateng, was the subject of a 2017 Internet article. While living in Atlanta, Georgia, Boateng met a relative of the Director of Ghana's Education Services. She later contacted the Director and began the process of establishing a school in Ghana. Boateng relocated to Ghana, and in 2006 she opened the Youth Institute of Science and Technology in a rural village in the Ashanti Region of

Ghana. Eventually Boateng opened a second school, and she is now the proprietor of a business that provides consultancy about repatriating to Ghana. In the article, Boateng noted that laws passed during the Fourth Republic prohibit foreigners from owning land in Ghana; they are mere leaseholders until they become citizens.[5] However, the process of becoming a citizen is also fraught with obstacles.

In 2015 the British Broadcasting Corporation published a printed article on a Detroit native named Chekesha Aidoo, who runs a school in Cape Coast, Ghana. The school, Akoma Academy, was founded by her late mother. The mission is to educate children in the Central Region of Ghana. Some of the children are educated free of charge, and for others Ms. Aidoo finds sponsors to pay their school fees.

Boateng, Wilkins, and Aidoo are three of many African Americans who have traveled to Ghana with a mission to educate children and adults in the impoverished country. I did have the pleasure of interviewing nine African-American educators in Ghana, trying to determine if this was a revival of the mission of the "Politicals," who endured many sacrifices to help President Nkrumah build the institutions of his fledgling country. Neither Boateng nor Wilkins nor Aidoo made mention of political motivations that led them to repatriate to Ghana. Nor did most of the expatriates whom I personally interviewed. There were, however, some exceptions. One educator who was involved in leftist politics in the U.S. stated a goal of "[c]hang[ing] the political milieu of Ghana," with a broader mission of "[t]ransforming the ideology of African people." This respondent also wishes to "become involved in the struggle against capitalism." In Ghana, the respondent believes, there is more opportunity for Black people involved in that struggle than there is in the U.S., because in Ghana "Black folks have the numbers." For now, however, this respondent is more focused on education than on activism.

The above respondent is very much the exception among expatriates, including those who are educators. One person, who has helped establish libraries in Ghana, expresses a feeling that providing political leadership would be an effort in futility. That respondent said that "Ghana isn't ready for any type of positive leadership. They do a lot of things that aren't right. Whomever they put in will be the same. But I do give kudos to President Mahama." This praise, however, was not an endorsement of the NDC. The respondent expressed a desire to become a citizen, but when pressed about voting in Ghana, the response was "I don't know." As for non-electoral political involvement, the respondent was not involved in the U.S., nor in Ghana. The respondent said, "I'm not gonna go out and carry signs. I didn't do it in the U.S. Carrying signs is not always conducive to change."

One educator could be classified as an "exile," but this individual has not been involved in Ghanaian politics. That respondent stated that the reason for leaving the U.S. was because of the persistent harassment of Black men by the law enforcement community in the U.S. The respondent made the following comment:

> I prefer Ghana. The contradictions are in the US, with the situations leading to the Black Lives Matter movement. There are things you have to deal with: police following you, and being followed in the stores.

While the level of harassment may indeed be far less than in the U.S., Ghana under the Fourth Republic does not wish to make itself a haven for repatriates who have had a police record. Ghana is not a revolutionary regime, such as that of Tanzania in the 1960s and 1970s, or Cuba since 1959. Political exiles who are also escaping criminal charges are not encouraged to enter, and persons applying for an extended residence in Ghana are required to submit a police report.[6]

Ghana is neither a haven for political refugees, nor is it totally exempt from abusive behavior by law enforcement officials. One educator related the following incident that took place during President Barack Obama's 2009 visit to Ghana, an incident in which Black Americans were specifically targeted:

> For example, when President Obama came to Ghana, the police came to eject the Diasporans from their seats. Some Diasporans refused to move. The police literally pushed Mrs. Kohain. The Diasporans refused to move. The cops had helmets, rifles and shields.

Mrs. Kohain is the wife of Kohain Nathanyah Halevi, an African American who is the director of the PANAFEST Foundation.[7]

An earlier quoted expatriate, one who is an educator, said the following about her work with youngsters:

> I walk a line that I'm very careful of. I taught students how to write letters, make public testimony. Not being a citizen I can't do this myself. We worked on a domestic violence bill, reproductive health, and child trafficking.

Some of the expatriates in Ghana were not teachers or educational administrators, and did not seek employment in educational institutions in Ghana, but they were involved in educational endeavors for Ghanaians. This they did by paying the "school fees," which many Ghanaians cannot afford for their children. One such benefactor is Earna Terefe-Kassa, who is originally from Detroit. Ms. Terefe-Kassa is an entrepreneur who pays school fees for more than sixty children.[8] Ms. Terefe-Kassa is also a retired educator with a master's degree in educational administration. She has volunteered to assist in the training of teachers in Ghana, but, to her dismay, local school officials have not responded to her offer.[9] By virtue of her generosity and her former career, this entrepreneur can also be classified as an educator.

# 5

# Organizations Founded by African American Expatriates

In this chapter, I examine three organizations that were formed with the purpose of providing assistance to African Americans living in Ghana: the African American Association of Ghana (AAAG), the Diaspora Africa Forum (DAF), and Fihankra International. The AAAG provides its members with social and cultural activities, and it is also committed to providing educational opportunities for Ghanaians. DAF serves to represent to the African Union those persons of African descent who live outside of the continent of Africa. Fihankra is a village in the Eastern Region of Ghana where African Americans have settled with the intention of permanent residency.

## The African American Association of Ghana

The oldest of the three organizations is the AAAG, which was founded in 1981 and became a formal organization in 1991. The organization was founded by African-American women who had moved to Ghana, and who were married to Ghanaian nationals. One of the members had the following to say about the origins of the AAAG:

> It began with women who came with Ghanaian husbands and were disturbed about their socio-cultural experiences. They married Ghanaians in the US. When they returned [to Ghana], they were placed in a subordinate position. They

often helped build houses and businesses in Ghana, but they had no inheritance rights. Their husbands sometimes took on other wives and supported them. Very few men were members of the organization.

The primary focus of the AAAG has been for members to provide each other with mutual support. A very active member of the organization said that when the organization was incorporated, "Most of the members were women married to Ghanaians. It was a social club, and it was formed to motivate each other."

Throughout the years of its existence, the AAAG has not emphasized political issues, though they have been involved in some political activities in the past. One very practical area in which they were involved in was in providing commodities for each other. In the early 1980s there were very few supermarkets in Ghana, so members helped organize trips to places where they could purchase products that were not available in stores and markets in the communities in which they resided. As the

Figure 3. Headquarters of the African American Association of Ghana (author's collection).

Ghanaian economy evolved, so did the AAAG, but they have retained their priority of providing support for expatriates as they cope with living thousands of miles from home. Many of today's members are males, such as myself. The organization sponsors social, educational, and cultural events. As one member told me, "The organization is to address cultural, social, economic, and spiritual integration of the U.S. emigres into African society." Another member said, "We are a social outlet, and we are involved in things that help us maintain our sanity here."

The social events sponsored by AAAG are varied. During the time that I was in Ghana, I was an active member of the organization. The regular meetings were held the third Sunday of each month, and there were also additional events, which included occasional weekend trips to Sanaa Lodge, a resort facility in the Central Region. This was a time for relaxation interspersed with book discussions. The trips were billed as "Books, Travel, and Wine." Another well-attended social event was a dance featuring music from the 1970s. This was held at the end of Black History Month. The proceeds from that dance went to charitable causes. In 2017 the proceeds were used to purchase equipment for two vocational educational facilities: the Opportunities Industrialisation Centre, and the Accra Rehabilitation Centre.[1]

At this stage in AAAG's history, there is a demonstrable commitment to providing education to Ghanaians. In addition to fundraising events such as the 1970s dance, AAAG provides scholarship money to select students enrolled at the University of Ghana. The Black History Month itineraries for 2016 and 2017 provide an example of the organization's commitment to educating Ghanaian students. In 2016 the following youth-centered educational activities were sponsored by the AAAG:[2]

1. Pan-African Youth program (February 5)

2. Film and discussion at the University of Ghana (February 14)

3. Film and discussion at BASICS International School (February 20)

4. Film and discussion (February 27).

In addition to the above activities (to which the youngsters were provided transportation to attend), there was a forum featuring educators (including myself) on Saturday, February 6.

The 2017 Black History Month agenda for AAAG included the following youth-related activities:[3]

1. High School Educational Program (February 3)
2. Children's Film and Discussion at BASICS International School (February 16)
3. Children's Film and Discussion (February 18).

As was the case in 2016, there was a forum of educators held on February 4, 2017.

The Black History Month activities for both years included cultural events. In 2016 there was an African-American style "soul food" luncheon, a tribute to the singer Natalie Cole (who had recently passed away); a "Spoken Word" event featuring poetry and song; and an African American-style worship service, featuring the AAAG Gospel Choir. The AAAG Choir returned in 2017 for another African-American-style worship service, and two weeks later there was a "Negro spirituals" concert.

In addition to the above programs, on April 4, 2016, I chaired a program honoring Dr. Martin Luther King, Jr., on the 48th anniversary of his death. That program featured speakers (including myself and other academicians), a film and discussion, and a solo by AAAG President Brenda Joyce, who is also an accomplished vocalist. Students from the University of Ghana were provided transportation to and from the event, and many were in attendance.

Many of the Black History Month events and the MLK remembrance event were made possible by the generous assistance provided by the United States Embassy in Ghana. AAAG has a very close relationship with the U.S. Embassy, and this underscores a fundamental difference between today's expatriates and the "Politicals" of six decades ago. The "Politicals" were persons who were on self-imposed exile from the United States, many of whom had no immediate intention of returning to the U.S. The AAAG is an organization that is supportive of the U.S., and this was especially true during the time that I was in Ghana, when Barack Obama was still President of the United States. In 2009 the AAAG held an event celebrating the inauguration of Barack Obama, and, as one AAAG officer put it, "We were in the forefront when Obama visited Ghana on July 11, 2009."

The AAAG is not a political organization, but that has not precluded it from becoming involved in some political issues, such as celebrating Obama's inauguration and visit. They have also been involved in the efforts to grant Black Americans the "Right of Abode," so that they can own land in Ghana, start businesses there, and remain in the country without paying the sizable annual fee that the Ghana Immigration Services requires of them.[4] The expatriates have not been successful in securing the right of abode, and the AAAG of late has not been involved in that effort. Two of my interviewees spoke of the AAAG's efforts to gain this right, and they both stated that the organization has moved away from that effort. As one member told me, the organization's involvement with the right of abode "depends on the leadership" at the time. The other informant said that the current leadership has moved in a different direction, with greater emphasis on educational events. A third informant noted that the organization shifts its focus to meet the needs of those who are members at that point in time. That informant praised the organization as being one that provides "a whole host of activities," and that "it serves the people who are involved at that particular time." One informant, however, is disappointed that the AAAG has not been more vociferous in advocating for a right of abode. This person, who is a member, said, "They talk about a right of abode, but they don't provide us with concrete help."

One informant, who is not a member, provided the most negative assessment of the organization. This person had no criticisms about the organization's lack of a political emphasis, but did not join the AAAG "because it's a social group who wants to hold onto American stuff. I came to Ghana to integrate into African culture." That statement does not accurately portray the purpose or the actual function of AAAG. During the short time that I lived in Ghana, I found the AAAG to be a vital organization, many of whose members have indeed "integrate[d] into African culture," and they have done that through matrimony. The AAAG is vital because it provides its members with a sense of community while they are thousands of miles away from people and places with which they are most familiar, including their close relatives. Expatriates have left behind siblings, parents, and children to make new lives for themselves in a strange land. Nearly all informants were very pleased about their decision to come to Ghana, but they experience the normal anxieties persons feel when they are away from the land of their nativity. They are forced to miss baptisms, graduations, weddings, and even funerals of loved ones. The AAAG was founded to provide support to people as they cope with being away from those dear to them and therefore missing important milestones in the lives of close friends and family members. My discussions with informants who are members of the organization confirm to me that the AAAG serves well the purpose for which it was founded. Through my participant observation, I was a beneficiary of the support provided by the AAAG. I was unable to attend the funeral of a close relative, and I had many adjustments to make while living in what seemed to be a different world than what I was accustomed to. I very much appreciated the interactions with people who could deeply empathize with my concerns. I agree with some informants that the AAAG is not passionately involved in political issues, such as lobbying parliament for a right of abode. However, when it comes to fulfilling its original purpose of providing support, it appears to me that the AAAG is meeting its goal.

## The Diaspora Africa Forum

The African-American-based expatriate organization that operates in the political arena is the Diaspora Africa Forum (DAF). DAF was launched by the African Union in 2005, and opened its doors as a diplomatic mission on July 1, 2007. I was present at the opening ceremony. The purpose of DAF is to provide diasporic Africans with diplomatic representation in the African Union (AU). Though the AU is headquartered in Addis Ababa, Ethiopia, the office of the DAF is at the W. E. B. Du Bois Centre, in Accra, Ghana. Dr. Erieka Bennett, the founder and head of DAF, has ambassadorial status with the AU, and goes by the title of Ambassador. Dr. Bennett's ambassadorial status was granted by the government of Ghana, where the DAF is registered as a non-governmental organization. According to the DAF's website, the purpose of the mission is "to support the African Union (AU) and member states towards the integration of Africans in the Diaspora while strengthening African Diaspora engagement in Ghana, specifically and continent wide, in general."[5] Previously the African Union was composed of five regions, representing the entire continent of Africa. The regions are Northern, Western, Central, Eastern, and Southern. The African Union now recognizes a sixth region, the Diaspora,[6] which is represented by Ambassador Bennett. This AU recognition is in line with Malcolm X's vision of an Organization of Afro-American Unity (OAAU) that would have a seat on the Organization of African Unity, which is now called the African Union.

The concept of an OAAU was formulated in May 1963 and had its origins within the African-American expatriate community in Ghana. Upon returning from a *hajj* in Mecca, Malcolm X took a trip to Ghana, and his itinerary was arranged by the expatriate community. In 1964, Malcolm X made a second trip to Africa and, upon returning, he formally established the OAAU. The ultimate purpose was formal recognition by the OAU.[7] That formal recognition did not occur until more than forty years later when the OAU, now called the AU, granted recognition to DAF as the representative of Diasporan Africans, and gave the DAF a seat on the AU, something that Malcolm X had envisaged.

One of my aims when I was in Ghana was to meet with Ambassador Bennett, interview her, and learn as much about the DAF as I did about AAAG. This proved to be very difficult. Dr. Bennett has an extremely busy schedule and is often out of the country. This is one of the disadvantages of having an office in a city (Accra) that is 3,800 miles away from the location (Addis Ababa) of the headquarters of the parent organization. Throughout the four months that I was based in Accra, I was never able schedule a meeting with Dr. Bennett. Unfortunately, DAF is not a membership-based organization, like AAAG. For if it were, I could have met with members and amassed as much information as I would have by meeting with Ambassador Bennett. DAF is not a social organization, but an office run by Ambassador Bennett. She had no Associate Director who could have provided me with valuable information about DAF. In order to learn about DAF, I had to rely upon the organization's website, and upon the words of the persons whom the DAF was founded to serve: the African-American expatriate community.

Two of my respondents did provide me with background information on the official and unofficial purposes of the Diaspora Africa Forum. One respondent volunteered the following information prior to my even mentioning the DAF in the interview:

> They are helping out people to get their visas straight so that they can stay here. . . . They seem to be on the up-and-up to help people who are working here and living here. They

give help for people who are behind in their visas. They try to [work with] representatives from different organizations in Ghana, to get Diasporans to work together.

Another interviewee, who is a member of the Ghana Caribbean Association had the following to say about DAF:

> DAF is an arm of the African Union, and represents what the AU now calls the sixth region of Africa. The Congressional Black Caucus helped spearhead it. Under President Kufuor, Ghana volunteered to host this region with an embassy. The second one will be in Senegal. Part of their mandate was to ease the travel difficulties, help people get an ECOWAS (Economic Community of West African States) visa.

Most of the other persons whom I interviewed were not as well aware of the accomplishments of the DAF, and most tended to believe that the organization falls far short of Malcolm X's vision for the OAAU. These are the words of one respondent:

> Malcolm X asked for an OAU seat for Diasporans, but he only had observer status. Brothers from New York City sat in that observer seat until the AU decided to give them ambassador status. Erieka . . . called a conference. It was held at a hotel, in which it was stated that Erieka would be the chair. . . . They were supposed to have meetings to design the structure for the seat, but they never had meetings. Next thing we know, Erieka was the Ambassador. And [the mission] went from [representing] Black Americans to include all diasporic Africans, even those who were born in Africa. She represents them. She says that she was designated by the Ghana government. How can the Ghana government make her the chair over the Diaspora seat? That's an AU position, not a Ghana seat.

Most of the respondents who spoke of DAF were unaware of what assistance the organization provided to individuals, and many questioned if DAF did indeed serve the expatriate community.

One thing that Dr. Bennett has been very successful in doing is fulfilling the social obligations that are demanded of an ambassador. But in so doing, some members of the expatriate community feel that she has neglected them. That is the sentiment expressed by this respondent:

> Erieka started that stuff. She has her little niche of people. She was very very close to Kufuor, and that's how she got that title of "Ambassador." I don't know what they do at DAF. She's had these dinners. She knows a lot of people. When she has these events, only certain people are invited.

Another respondent was unaware of what DAF does for the expatriate community. Like the previous respondent, this interviewee said, "I've never been invited to become involved." When I asked another about the DAF, the respondent said, "I've heard of it. I wanted to talk to Erieka. I know that the Diaspora is the 6th region of the AU. [Erieka] wouldn't give me any information." This informant was sent to the DAF's office for more information. I followed the suggestion to go to the DAF office, but I found very little information that could not have been secured from DAF's website.

One respondent spoke to me about a request that was made to DAF concerning a pressing issue in the United States. In 2014, the topic of police brutality in the U.S. was brought to the forefront after the killing of an unarmed Black man by the Ferguson, Missouri Police Department. Some of the residents of Ferguson asked the expatriates in Ghana to help raise Africans' awareness of Black Americans' tortured relationship with law enforcement officials. Expatriates in Ghana tried to contact DAF, but they received no response, neither by postal mail nor by electronic mail. The respondent who relayed this information to me had the following to say about DAF: "I know what they're supposed to do, but I don't know what they do." The respondent did, however, acknowledge that Ambassador Bennett and DAF "have done things for African women, and for education in Ghana." This informant, like others whom I interviewed, knew little more about the office other than the name of the Ambassador and the location of the mission.

This situation exemplifies a dilemma. DAF was established as a diplomatic mission, and its director as an ambassador, but it is connected neither to a state nor to a government in exile. In most situations ambassadors represent a recognized state or, in rarer cases, a stateless people who reside in a disputed territory over which they desire sovereignty. Dr. Bennett is designated as an ambassador over a people with neither a state nor a region that they claim dominion over. She was not given her designation by a government that presides over the people she purportedly represents, neither is there a "government-in-exile" that exists to advocate in the international arena on behalf of her constituents. Nevertheless, she is recognized as an ambassador, and as such is expected to perform the functions of an ambassador. Those functions include hosting dignitaries from different countries, and boosting the image of the people whom she has been chosen to represent. In these ambassadorial capacities, Dr. Bennett has performed her duties with excellence. Though she has been criticized for not inviting many expatriates to the events that she hosts, no other ambassadors have comprehensive guest lists for formal occasions. She has also adopted a cause and used her status as an ambassador to promote it. That cause is the condition of African women in the Diaspora and on the continent, whose lot she is working toward improving.[8] While her many trips do not address the concerns of individual Diasporans, they do bolster the image and reputation of DAF. That is the precise role of a diplomat and Dr. Bennett has fulfilled that particular role.

The dilemma is that Ambassador Bennett represents no state, no territory, nor an easily defined group of people. Diasporans have no single recognized group. Unlike the Palestinian Authority, they do not have a disputed territorial region, and unlike the "Free French" during World War II, or the African National Congress prior to 1994, there is no "shadow government" that can be recognized as their representative and that can appoint ambassadors. With no governing structure, official or unofficial, some expatriates residing in Ghana are expecting DAF to perform the functions of a governing entity, or at least the functions of an embassy. DAF is neither a government nor an embassy; it is a small diplomatic mission, and it does not have the budget nor does it have the authority to meet the expectations of some of the expatriates. Dr. Bennett has no large staff that can meet with individual expatriates and provide constituency services. Nor is she the employee of a tax-supported government that can assign tasks to her. She neither has the time nor the mandate to meet with individual constituents and address all of their concerns before the African Union. Dr. Bennett's salary and diplomatic credentials were provided by forces external to the group she is designated to represent. Therein lies the dilemma. She is expected to perform the functions of a government official, but the group she represents before the AU played no role in making her an ambassador, nor does this group pay taxes that provide her salary, as is typically the case with an ambassador. The AU appointed Dr. Bennett to serve as an ambassador,[9] which is precisely what she has done since 2007, but expatriates, who played no role in her appointment, would like her to provide some of the services of a governmental entity. The only way for such to occur would be for Diasporans themselves to establish an organization and provide continuous and generous support. DAF is not such an organization; it is a subsidiary of the African Union, and receives its support from the AU.[10]

## Fihankra International

One African-American organization in Ghana has limited jurisdiction over a small swath of land in eastern Ghana. The organization is called Fihankra International. The Fihankra community exemplifies African-American involvement in traditional politics, the politics enmeshed in African customs that predated colonialism. Fihankra had its origins in December 1994, when some Ghanaian and Nigerian chiefs met in Accra to participate in a ceremony in which they atoned for their ancestors' participation in the Atlantic slave trade. The rituals included "purifying" an animal skin and a stool. This represented an apology on behalf of the actions of chiefs from northern Ghana (where chiefs sit on skins) and southern Ghana (where chiefs sit on stools).[11] The ceremony was attended by over 3,000 people, including some government officials.[12]

One of those in attendance was a Detroit native named Kwadwo Oluwale Akpan (formerly Gregory Simmons). At the time of the establishment of Fihankra, Akpan had been living in Ghana for three years. Prior to that, while still in the U.S., he had been a leader of the Pan-African Congress–USA. At the atonement ceremony Akpan was appointed as paramount chief (Omanhene) over Fihankra, a community that was to be developed in the Akwamu area in eastern Ghana. In 1997 Akpan's organization, Fihankra International, was given jurisdiction over a 30,000-acre territory in what became known as Fihankra, which is translated as "When leaving home, no goodbyes were said." That reflects the experiences of the ancestors of Diasporic Africans. From 1997 to 2008 the paramount (ruling) chief of the village was Nana Akpan, who was entrusted as the custodian of the land, with the mandate to establish a settlement of persons from the Diaspora.[13]

Chief ("Nana") Akpan was made a traditional leader of Fihankra, and his paramountcy incorporated the traditions of Akans and non-Akans. Fihankra has both a stool and a skin for its chief. The honorific title "Nana" is the Akan word for chief, but Nana Akpan adopted a patrilineal mode of succession, which is the practice of non-Akans.[14] One of the residents of Fihankra gave a brief description of this Black American embrace of African traditions:

> The African Americans have established their own tribe, called Kɔfobiafo, which means "One who has been taken and returned." Though their chief has the Akan title "Nana," they chose a patrilineal system. . . . We wrote up our own chieftaincy system and rules for how our community functions."

Chiefs from the Akwamu Traditional Area, in eastern Ghana, allocated the land to Fihankra International. The plans were for the village to have medical clinics, schools, lecture halls, recreational facilities, and libraries.[15] While the results of this economic development would obviously be long-term, Fihankra International's control over the land would only last for fifty years. In Ghana, non-citizens are given a 50-year lease on the land, which is one-half of the lease period for citizens.[16] But despite these restrictions, the community began to flourish. Though they were offered 30,000 acres, they accepted 310 to begin with, but that number was reduced to 268. According to a prominent resident, the size of the plot was reduced because "they were duped out of 42 acres." At its peak, in 2005, there were fifteen to twenty residents, and, according to the former resident whom I interviewed, they were successful in making healthcare available to the persons living in the nearby vicinity:

> They helped enhance the healthcare there by providing eyeglasses, prescriptions, surgeries. They had four medical clinics between 1996 and 1998, and more than 4,000 patients. Most doctors joined in and dropped their fees. Dr. Nkrumah Mills was head of the hospital. Doctors from other hospitals joined in and did the work for free.

Nana Akpan presided over Fihankra until his death on May 30, 2008, while he was on a business trip in the neighboring country of Togo. His death precipitated a controversy. The chief who originally leased the land to Fihankra International, the Akwamuhene (chief of the Akwamu area), passed away before Fihankrahene (chief of Fihankra) Akpan. Nana Appiah Nti was the successor of the Akwamuhene; Nti and his supporters on the Akwamu Traditional Council refused to recognize the legitimacy of Nana Akpan, and would not allow Nana Akpan's remains to return to Fihankra for burial, as is the custom for a chief. A traditional burial in Fihankra would have accorded recognition of Akpan as the sovereign of Fihankra. The Traditional Council also refused to recognize Nana Akpan's son, Goloi Osakwe Akpan, as Fihankrahene, nor did they recognize Akpan's widow Majewa as Queen Mother, or Fihankrahemaa. Nana Akpan's initial enstoolment, involving use of both Akan and non-Akan traditions, could be positively viewed by some as the evolution of a new tradition, while others might see it as a violation of long-standing traditions. At this point the latter viewpoint appears to prevail among traditional rulers (chiefs) in Ghana, such as Nana Appiah Nti.

Nana Nti was supported by some of the African-American residents of Fihankra, who accused the Akpan family of mismanagement of the village's funds, and therefore were opposed to Goloi Osakwe's accession to his father's stool and skin. In October 2014 the Chieftaincy Minister, Dr. Henry Seidu Daanaa, ordered the arrest of Goloi and Majewa Akpan for allegedly assuming the titles of "Chief" and "Queen Mother" without authorization. The Akpans' lawyer insisted that they never took on traditional titles, but were merely the custodians of the stool and skin of the deceased Fihankrahene. Finally, in January 2016 the charges were dropped by an Accra circuit court.[17]

Eight months before the dismissal of the charges, the dispute came to a tragic head. In May 2015 two elderly female supporters of the Akpan family were bludgeoned to death and buried in a shallow grave in Fihankra. Six persons were arrested, including Nana Appiah Nti and three African Americans who were opposed to the Akpan Family. The person accused of physically carrying out the murder later confessed to acting alone,[18] and the charges against the others were withdrawn.[19] The killer, who had no known ties to the African-American community, also confessed to three earlier unrelated murders in Ghana.[20]

My interviews were conducted less than one year after these heinous crimes, and some of the respondents were close to the victims, while others had some connection with Fihankra. One respondent, who was very close to Nana Akpan, expressed regret that the support that traditional leaders gave to the settlers back in 1997 is no longer accorded to them. These are the words of that settler:

> Nana Akpan's dream was to be able to establish the community, and the chiefs in their own recognition entrusted him with the land. He established relations with the chiefs before the organization [Fihankra International] came about, before the beginning of the development of the Fihankra community. But that support from the traditional chiefs doesn't exist anymore. I have heard that some have passed away, and some new chiefs didn't want to recognize our sovereignty over the land.

The above respondent has moved away from Fihankra, as have many other settlers since the tragedies occurred. This respondent described the organization of Fihankra International as being "in a dormant stage."

I did meet with expatriates who were unsupportive of the Akpan family and of his son becoming the chief. One expatriate resident of Cape Coast said the following about Nana Akpan's widow:

> Majewa followed the same line as her husband; she said that the land belongs to her family. Some of us in Cape Coast took a stand, and Majewa agreed that some mistakes were made. But when it came time to change things, she was stuck.

An expatriate who resides in Accra criticized Nana Akpan because this informant believed that, "Nana Akpan tried to put his Liberian adopted son up as chief. [His son] had no tie to us."

Though Kwadwo Oluwale Akpan was the only U.S.-born African American serving as an omanhene, many others have been accorded the title of chief. Some foreigners have committed themselves to assisting villages in development projects. In recognition of this commitment, they have been installed as development chiefs for the villages that they adopted. In 1985 the king of the Ashanti people (the Asantehene) Otumfuo Opoku Ware II authorized the creation of a position called the Nkɔsuohene, which translates into the words "Development (Nkɔsuo) Chief (hene)." When the benefactor is a female, the position is called the "Nkɔsuohemaa," which means "Development Queen Mother." Persons who receive such an honor are given the traditional royal trappings, provided with an African name, clothed in royal garments, and seated on a carved stool. They are also entrusted with the responsibility of executing development projects in the village.[21] Among those prominent Diasporans who have been "enstooled" as development chiefs or queen mothers are musicians Isaac Hayes, Rita Marley, and Stevie Wonder; academics John Henrick Clarke, Molefi Asante, and Leonard Jeffries; psychologist Na'im Akbar; minister Jeremiah Wright; and Washington, DC, former mayor Anthony Williams.[22] The practice of installing development chiefs has spread beyond the Ashantis and to other ethnic groups in order to encourage the establishment of projects to help develop villages throughout Ghana.

None of the persons whom I interviewed has yet been seated as a development chief, but one female has been offered to become a Nkɔsuohemaa. This prospective queen mother has not yet agreed to accept the position. She gave the following reason for her reticence:

> I am taking this slow because it is a lot of responsibility. And the area and region have significant historical relevance. . . . So I am taking the time to learn what I need to learn to serve the people.

The respondent said the following about how Ghanaians' view the enstoolment of African Americans as chiefs and queen mothers:

> This title can also be used to make a mockery of us. Ghanaians often laugh about the idea of foreigners becoming queen mothers and chiefs.

T. C. McCaskie, in his study if the Ashanti culture, also spoke of how some Ashantis have ridiculed the enstoolment of American Nkɔsuohenes/hemaas:

> In private, many Asante chiefs angrily mock Africans from the diaspora who think they have somehow returned home and been reintegrated because they wear cloth, speak greetings in Twi and buy Nkɔsuo stools. Painful though it is to say, and no one seems willing to say it, many Asante office holders

regard returnees from the diaspora as unwelcome descendants of slaves, as well as being people who proclaim themselves to be African but all too often behave like stereotypical "ugly Americans."[23]

One of my respondents spoke of this division among Ashanti chiefs in regard to giving recognition of African Americans. When Ghana's National House of Chiefs held the 1994 ceremony atoning for slavery, it was supported by the head of the House of Chiefs, Nana Oduro Nimapau II. Nana Nimapau was an Ashanti but, according to one of my informants, the atonement ceremony did not have widespread support among other Ashanti chiefs. My informant believes that this may be due to the fact that Ashantis were heavily involved in the Atlantic slave trade. According to this informant, Nana Nimapau was "vehemently opposed by the other Ashantis."

Perhaps one consolation for those opposed to awarding honorary chieftaincies to foreigners is that these individuals are not eligible to become paramount chiefs, and do not have the right to a seat in the National House of Chiefs. The only possible exception in regard to paramount chiefs was Nana Kwadwo Oluwole Akpan, who was an Nkɔsuohene before he became an omanahene. However, even as the paramount chief of Fihankra, Akpan was denied in his request to become a member of the Ghana National House of Chiefs.[24] At present, the only way in which African Americans can enter the traditional political structure of Ghana is to become a powerless Nkɔsuohene or Nkɔsuohemaa.

# 6

# Summary and Outlook

## Avoidance of Political Activity

When I began the research for this project, my goal was to explore the political involvement of African-American expatriates residing in Ghana. I set out to learn about their political activities and partisanship in the U.S. and in their adopted country. What I discovered was that most were active in U.S. politics, to some degree, and that they heavily favored the Democratic Party. Their partisanship was no surprise, since African Americans are the demographic group that exhibits the highest level of support for the Democratic Party. What was somewhat surprising was to learn that those who have immigrated to Ghana have been, for the most part, apolitical in that country. They have refrained from political involvement, even in those avenues of participation that are available to them. As non-citizens they are unable to vote in Ghanaian elections, but the open democracy of Ghana does allow them to participate in non-electoral political activities. Even so, most expatriates seemed to have abandoned political activity after they became residents of Ghana. While most are not politically active, some have expressed their partisan leanings in Ghana. What I found even more surprising than their non-involvement was that many either have no partisan preference or have expressed support for the New Patriotic Party, the right-of-center party that emulates the U.S.'s Republican Party. I had assumed that most would support the National Democratic Congress, which occupies the same ideological space as the Democratic Party that African Americans are so very loyal to. Moreover, the NDC presents itself as the successor to Kwame Nkrumah, who was one of the first Africans to initiate a high level of outreach to African Americans. The first generation of African-American migrants to Ghana, those who entered during the Nkrumah regime, were strongly supportive of Nkrumah, so I assumed that this current generation would likewise support the NDC rather than the NPP, the successor to the original anti-Nkrumahist parties.

The African-American expatriates of the 1950s and 1960s were not only partisan (in support of Nkrumah's Convention People's Party), but they were also politically active, so much so that they were called "the Politicals." Such is not the case with the African-American expatriates of the twenty-first century. After interviewing my respondents, I have come to understand why the two groups of expatriates are so different concerning political priorities. The changing priorities of African-American expatriates is not a reflection of a change in the objectives of African Americans in the United States. The difference is not in the universe of African Americans, but in the groups who have immigrated to Ghana. During the First Republic, Kwame Nkrumah issued an invitation to African Americans to come to Ghana to assist him as he helped develop what became the world's third Black republic. He wanted not only their technical expertise, but also their ideas. Particularly welcome were dissidents, such as W. E. B. Du Bois and Julian Mayfield. Those who moved to Ghana during the days of the First Republic were politically mobilized when they arrived, hence many assumed positions in the CPP government.

Decades earlier, a somewhat similar situation existed among certain immigrant groups who came to the United States. While many came for economic opportunities that existed in the developing and expanding country, others came as political refugees escaping persecution in their homelands. The latter group of immigrants, and their offspring, became heavily involved in political activism in the United States. Ashkenazic Jews, who fled persecution in Russia and Eastern Europe, came to the United States and immersed themselves into the political system. Often, due to language barriers, the first-generation immigrants were restricted in their political involvement, but their children and grandchildren, many of whom grew up in squalid tenements, became politicians, government officials, and social activists. Among such notable Jews were Louis Brandeis, Arthur Goldberg, Jacob Javits, Edward Koch, and Bella Abzug.[1] Another group of immigrants who fled political persecution in Europe was the "Forty-Eighters," socially progressive Germans who left Europe after the failure of the 1848 revolution in Europe. Many of the Forty-Eighters settled in the Midwest, where they and their descendants contributed to the progressive agrarian politics of that region. Three prominent Forty-Eighters were U.S. Senator Carl Schurz,[2] U.S. Representative Lorenz Brentano,[3] and Wisconsin Interim Governor Edward Salomon.[4] On the other end of the political spectrum were Cuban refugees who fled the communist takeover of their island. Cuban Americans helped make the Republican Party the dominant party in the state of Florida, and many became nationally known politicians. Republicans Marco Rubio, Ileana Ros-Lehtinen, Carlos Curbelo, and Mario Diaz-Balart, are members of Congress who had their political origins in south Florida.[5] Jews, Forty-Eighters, and Cubans became overrepresented among those involved in service to the United States government.

Another group of political refugees who (along with their immediate descendants) contributed to the political development of the United States is Irish Americans, who first began arriving to the U.S. in large numbers during the 1840s. Some might disagree with the characterization of Irish immigrants as political refugees rather than economic refugees. Though many arrived destitute, having escaped starvation in their homeland, they were indeed political refugees. If economics had been their sole motivation to escape Ireland, they could have more easily traveled to England, which was much closer to Ireland, and which would not have required the sacrifices experienced in a trans-Atlantic voyage. Many indeed did settle in England and made the port city of Liverpool a heavily Irish city on the English coast.[6] A far greater number wanted to leave the British Isles and settle in a country with an established republican democracy, and where their rights as a religious minority were guaranteed. These politically mobilized settlers and their children became heavily involved in municipal governments in the northeast and north-central regions of the United States, despite the discrimination they faced as impoverished Catholics.

African-American refugees who fled to Ghana had an advantage over the previously mentioned groups in the U.S. The first-generation of immigrants to Ghana moved to a country where they had lifelong fluency in the official language, which is English. That is why well-educated African Americans, such as Shirley Graham Du Bois, could move to Ghana and help establish the Ghana Broadcasting System. The major obstacle they faced in serving Ghana was the short duration of the First Republic. The 1966 demise of the First Republic marked the end of African-American involvement in Ghana's government.

When Flight Lieutenant Jerry John Rawlings took over Ghana in the early-1980s, his junta, the Provisional National Defence Council, appeared to resume Nkrumah's invitation to African Americans, an invitation that had been dormant for sixteen years. There was, however, a major difference. Nkrumah was a revolutionary pan-Africanist, while Rawlings was a neoliberal pan-Africanist. Rawlings's invitation was not to refugees fleeing racial oppression and political persecution. After the PNDC made the abrupt change from socialism to free-market economics, Rawlings's priority was for immigrants to come and assist in economic development. There was no desire for any group, foreign or Ghanaian, to join the PNDC in managing the affairs of government. The PNDC was a military junta that operated in a dictatorial fashion; they wanted no outside advice on running the country. Rawlings wanted investors, not exiles. When the PNDC recast itself as the NDC (National Democratic Congress), elections were held, but expatriates were not allowed to take part in the electoral process.

The Jerry Rawlings of the Fourth Republic was very different from the youthful junior military officer who seized the reins of government in 1979. Rawlings first burst onto the scene as a revolutionary, espousing some of the socialist rhetoric of the late Kwame Nkrumah. His first junta, the Armed Forces Revolutionary Council, held office for three months and then allowed the installation of a democratically elected civilian government. Two years later Rawlings launched a coup against that same civilian government and again expressed his socialist leanings. In less than two years, however, he abruptly ended his experiment with socialism and succumbed to the will of the international financial institutions. In 1983 Rawlings implemented free-market reforms, yet he still sang the praises of Kwame Nkrumah. Despite these praises, he implemented policies greatly different from those of Nkrumah, including the policies toward African Americans.

Rawlings's 1983 about-face and the departure from socialism were the result of international factors over which Rawlings had no control. The world's geopolitical situation had drastically changed between 1957, when Nkrumah ushered Ghana to independence, and 1982, when the PNDC became entrenched in office. When Nkrumah assumed power, leaders of some developing nations believed that they could depend upon massive support from the Soviet Union and eastern-bloc nations, and that this support would be sufficient for them to attain their goals. Nkrumah and other socialists thought that they could ignore the West and still sustain economic growth. In the 1980s it was becoming increasingly clear that the eastern-bloc nations had little to offer. Ghana, Jamaica, and other countries that had experimented with socialism were forced to turn to the West for financial support, which usually came in the form of loans. In order to qualify for these loans, the leaders were required to implement structural adjustment programs, which necessitated massive budget cuts. The only way to counter the effects of budget cuts was to stimulate economic growth. One ingredient for such growth was to secure the investment of entrepreneurs, both foreign and domestic. That is the route that the PNDC, the subsequent NDC, and the NPP have taken since 1983. A post-Cold War Ghana needs the support of African-American entrepreneurs, not of African-American dissidents.

Most of the expatriates seem to be meeting the expectations of the Ghanaian government. They and/or their spouses are establishing business enterprises and contributing to the economy of Ghana, while avoiding local politics. Just as future President Akufo Addo told me in that October 2015 meeting, "They are a very productive group of people." Many of them immigrated to Ghana to achieve economic success and, in pursuit of that goal, they have not allowed themselves to become sidetracked by involvement in politics. This is not to imply that there is not a selfless spirit among the expatriates. Some of them have not come to establish businesses, but to work as educators, and even the entrepreneurs have made their contributions to the education of Ghanaian children and young adults. In this regard, they are similar to the earlier generation of expatriates. Both waves of immigrants to Ghana include many people who have a desire to contribute their intellectual resources to their adopted country.

## African-American Partisanship in the United States and Ghana

The apparent irony is that many of the current generation of expatriates were politically active in the U.S., and usually they belonged to the Democratic Party. In Ghana the NDC is the closest to a Democratic Party equivalent, so I had hypothesized that those expatriates who did show a political inclination would support the NDC. This I found not to be the case. From my conversations with my respondents, I discovered that those who supported the NDC were far outnumbered by those who had no preference or who supported the NPP. Much of this has to do with the similarity between the political structures of the two countries. In both Ghana and the U.S. each legislative district is represented by only one member of Parliament (or Congress). With single-member districts, there is little chance for persons from smaller parties to gain representation, so nearly all legislators belong to one of two major parties. This provides a disincentive for parties to move away from the political center. As a result, there is *partisan convergence* on most major issues. The United States has a much longer history than Ghana, so I will briefly discuss the phenomenon of partisan convergence in the U.S. For much of the history of the United States, the parties did not differ on most issues. Where they differed was on the basis of the ethnic groups and geographic regions that aligned with the parties. The exceptions have been the Civil War/Reconstruction era and the Great Depression. During the 1860s and 1870s, the Democratic Party was popular in the South, so large factions of that party supported secession in the 1860s and opposed Reconstruction in the 1870s. This was a period of partisan divergence. By the 1880s the Republican Party had abandoned the program of Reconstruction, and the partisan status quo returned. That was a status quo whereby the parties converged on policy but differed by the ethnic, religious, and geographic groups who supported the parties. The Republican Party was the party of the industrial northeast, the Midwest, and of non-Southerners of Anglo Saxon and Protestant descent. The Democratic Party was supported by immigrant stock voters, Catholics, and White Southerners. There were very few ideological differences between the parties.

The 1880s to the 1920s was an era of partisan convergence in the United States, but it was disrupted by the Great Depression. With unemployment surpassing 20 percent, wages declining, and banks shuttering their doors, the public had moved leftward on economic issues. The Democratic Party, which was longing to regain control of the presidency, moved leftward along with the general public. This led to a realignment that gave the Democrats control over the executive and legislative branches of the U.S. government. Flanigan and Zingale describe the Depression-era realignment as an "across-the-board" change because all regions and demographic groups increased their support toward the Democratic Party.[7] This led to the landslide victory of Democrat Franklin Roosevelt in 1932, and an even greater landslide reelection in 1936. By 1940 the parties had converged, and the Republican nominee for president, Wendell

Willkie, who had very recently been a Democrat, was ideologically closer to Roosevelt than he was to many members of the Republican Party.[8]

Beginning in the late-1940s there was a dealignment, in which many voters moved back toward the Republican Party. One exception, however, was African Americans. They never went back to the Republican Party, and over the next two decades they increased their support for the Democratic Party. Currently, in U.S. presidential elections, around 90 percent of African Americans vote Democratic. The reason why African Americans stayed with the Democrats after the Depression-era realignment faded was because in 1948 the Democratic Party began to support civil rights, while the Republican Party began pursuing a "Southern strategy" of moving away from civil rights support in order to gain the votes of White Southerners. In 1964, the year that the U.S. Congress passed the Civil Rights Act, the Democratic nominee for president was the incumbent who had signed the Act, while his Republican opponent had voted against the Act. Though the two parties converged on the other major issue of the day—the Cold War that had become "hot" in Southeast Asia—they were very divergent on civil rights issues. This has been the situation since 1964. As the general ideology of the U.S. public has shifted rightward on many issues, so has the Democratic Party, especially during the 1990s under President Bill Clinton. Nevertheless, the Democratic Party has not moved rightward on the issue of equal rights for African Americans. On this issue the parties greatly diverge, and this is why the Democrats maintain such a high level of support among Black Americans.

In Ghana, there are no civil rights issues of particular importance to African Americans, so there is nothing to distinguish the two parties in the eyes of expatriates. The parties do have different ethnic bases, but this means little to Black Americans who belong to none of the tribes that make up the parties' coalitions. With the parties having similar platforms on most salient issues, and with there being no U.S.-style civil rights issues, expatriates see little or no difference between the NDC and the NPP. Their alliance with the parties is more likely based upon the affiliations of their spouses or their neighbors. It has nothing to do with the resemblance of the NDC and the NPP to parties back in the United States.

The political landscape was different during the days of the First Republic, and that is why most expatriates then favored Nkrumah's

Convention People's Party. Kwame Nkrumah made a strong outreach toward African Americans. He had received his undergraduate education at an HBCU, where he affiliated with a Black American fraternity. In 1951 Nkrumah returned to the U.S. and spoke before a predominantly Black crowd in New York City.[9] In 1958 he returned to the U.S. as the leader of an independent Ghana. He traveled to Harlem and addressed a crowd of 100,000, most of whom were Black Americans.[10] He also addressed Black Americans in Chicago and Philadelphia, and invited them to come to Ghana to provide their expertise.[11] Nkrumah returned to Harlem in 1960 and addressed a crowd in front of the historic Hotel Theresa.[12] Nkrumah's principal rival during that period, J. B. Danquah, did not make such overtures to Black America, which is why most African Americans in Ghana were staunchly supportive of the CPP.

In today's Ghana, neither party can be seen as more supportive of the African-American expatriate community. It was Rawlings who invited Black Americans, but it was under the NPP administration that the Joseph Project was launched, as was the Diaspora Africa Forum, both with the support of President Kufuor. The call for a "right of abode" and dual citizenship has been unheeded by NPP and NDC governments. Neither of the major parties of the Fourth Republic can claim to be the most supportive of Diasporans from the U.S. Another major difference between the days of the First Republic and those of the Fourth Republic is that during the First Republic the repatriates came directly in response to the invitation of Ghana's head of state. Only one of the respondents stated that the motivation to move to Ghana was Rawlings' invitation, and most respondents came either to invest in businesses or to serve as educators. This explains why the current repatriates do not have the dedication to the NDC that the earlier repatriates had toward Nkrumah's CPP.

## The Vital Role of Organizations

Two African-American organizations that I examined—the AAAG and the DAF—are not, at this time, pressing the government of Ghana to move on the issues of dual citizenship or a "right of abode." This avoidance by the AAAG is due to the priorities of the membership of the organization, and to the mission of the organization. My conversations with members of the AAAG clarified the purpose of the Association. The AAAG currently provides its members with social activities, promotes awareness of

Black American culture, and helps create educational opportunities for Ghanaians. At this current time, the membership is pleased with pursuing these aims, rather than lobbying the government or supporting one Ghanaian political faction over another. The members of the expatriate community prefer to avoid politics in Ghana, and the AAAG reflects that preference.

The same can be said of the Diaspora Africa Forum. Very few members of the expatriate community are aware of the work performed by DAF, but this may be due to the fact that DAF is an extremely unique office. It is a diplomatic mission representing a very large group of people (Diasporans from the Caribbean, the U.S., South America, and those Diasporans who were born in Africa) who, as a group, have no defined territory, no government, and no central organization to clarify its mission. This is a very rare type of diplomatic mission in that it was created by entities (the AU and the government of Ghana) that are external to the persons the mission is mandated to represent. This is quite confusing, which is the reason why so few expatriates know the purpose of DAF. Perhaps as time progresses DAF will be able to point out its accomplishments since it was created in 2007.

The third organization that I looked at was Fihankra International, which provided Black Americans an entrée into traditional politics. It was through Fihankra that African Americans tried to establish themselves as a separate tribe, the Kɔfobiafo, with a chief, Nana Kwadwo Oluwale Akpan. Unfortunately for his supporters, his legitimacy was not accepted by the National House of Chiefs, which denied him a seat. There was also a question as to the legitimacy of his successor, Goloi Osakwe Akpan, who was rejected by Ghanaian chiefs and by one segment of the Fihankra community. The brutal and tragic murders of two of the matriarchs of Fihankra have led to the gradual demise of this attempt to place African Americans into the traditional political structure in Ghana. The only semblance of African-American involvement in traditional politics is the concept of the Nkɔsuohene and Nkɔsuohemaa. These positions were created, not for the purpose of integrating non-Ghanaians into the traditional political structure, but to encourage these foreigners to help villages pursue development projects. This is a village-level equivalent of Rawlings's invitation to African Americans. Non-Ghanaians are asked to help develop, but not to help govern. Foreigners' resources are desired, but these benefactors are barred from any decision-making responsibilities.

The limitations on African Americans participating in Ghanaian politics are likely to last for the foreseeable future. There is no prospect for a new constitution that could put an end to the NDC/NPP duopoly, so there will be no pro-Diaspora pan-African party similar to the original CPP. One of my respondents advocated for "a complete revolution," brought about peacefully by educating people about other options. Such a change, no matter how peacefully and lawfully done, will not occur in Ghana, a country whose current republic has garnered international praise. Ghana's duopolistic Fourth Republic is among the most stable in Africa. The constitution has been in operation for twenty-six years, with no coups, no coup attempts, no civil wars. Since the Fourth Republic was instituted, there have been seven peaceful elections, three of which have resulted in a change of ruling party. Of the fifty-four countries in Africa, only four others (Benin, Cabo Verde, Mauritius, and Sao Tome and Principe) can boast of such stability. It is this stability that will continue to attract expatriates. Persons wishing to move to Africa to retire, to establish a business, or to launch an educational career can find no country that is more predictable than Ghana. Ghana is less welcoming to those who wish to become involved in political activism, or who wish join the traditional political structure (chieftaincy). The age of the exiles ended on February 24, 1966, but Ghana's desire for entrepreneurs and educators continues as we approach the third decade of the twenty-first century.

## Outlook for the Future

The Republic of Ghana has yet to develop a mechanism whereby African descendants from the Caribbean and the North American mainland can repatriate and receive the rights enjoyed by Ghanaian citizens. If such a measure has not been passed after a quarter of a century of the Fourth Republic, it is unlikely to happen in the near future. But it is the longevity of the civilian-ruled and democratic Fourth Republic that makes Ghana a popular destination for Black people from the diaspora who wish to repatriate to the continent of their ancestors. Ghana is one of the most stable countries on the continent, and this bodes well for persons who wish to establish residence there. When compared with many other countries, immigrants are well received in Ghana. Unlike in Europe, there are no movements dedicated to eradicating the country of immigrants.

Black Americans wishing to move to Ghana have far less to fear in that regard than those who wish to move to Europe. They are very unlikely to find themselves victims of organized violence. A major reason for this is that they cannot be perceived as an economic threat. Those African Americans who migrate to Ghana today are primarily entrepreneurs who are contributing to the economy, while a smaller number are educators providing a vital service. Many of those who are not involved in teaching are nonetheless contributing to the education of Ghanaians either through fundraising or outright payments of students' school fees. That is why President Akufo-Addo can assert that "They are a very productive group of people."

Another reason why African Americans are somewhat welcome in Ghana is that at this point their numbers are very low, and mostly confined to the Greater Accra region.[13] The approximately 3,000 African Americans are one one-hundredth of one percent of the population, and that percentage is not increasing at a very rapid rate. Ghanaians have no reason to worry that African Americans will damage their cultural integrity. Moreover, unlike countries in Europe, Ghana has no centuries-long history of having one established culture. European countries are nation-states, where the states were established around existing ethnic groups. Such is not the case in Africa, where the state boundaries were established by Europeans during the Conference of Berlin. The delegates at that conference did not take into account ethnic divisions, hence most of the colonies that they created were multi-ethnic entities. Those ethnically diverse colonies became modern independent states, within whose boundaries were people of different languages, religions, and traditions. The capital cities of Africa, including Accra, include migrants from all regions of their respective countries, hence multiculturalism is an accepted reality. Not one of my interviewees spoke of being harassed or threatened due to his or her foreigner status. Despite not being able to vote in elections, and despite the restrictions in land ownership and the opening of small businesses, the repatriates with whom I spoke do not feel unwelcome in Ghana, and most have no intention of returning to the U.S. to live. For the foreseeable future, immigrants in Ghana will enjoy a much safer existence than immigrants in economically developed countries. That is the outlook for the future for repatriates residing in Ghana.

The outlook for the future for this particular study of repatriates is equally positive, in my estimation. This book will add to the literature on immigration, but from a very different perspective than most of the current work on that topic. Most studies on immigration, both academic and journalistic, look at the experiences of immigrants living in nations that receive large numbers of entrants from other countries. This study looks at the experience of emigrants who leave a country that receives large numbers of immigrants, and who settle in a country that has been a source of emigrants leaving to move to economically developed countries. If, for some reason, the number of African-American repatriates grows by a substantial margin in the coming years, the findings of this study will be valuable in the future for researchers who wish to compare the experience of African-American repatriates in the first twenty years of the twenty-first century with those who reside in Ghana at that later point when their presence will be much more noticeable. Currently, however, this is a rare study that compares two phases of immigration of people from an industrialized nation to a nation whose economy is in an earlier stage of economic development.

# Notes

## Introduction

1. Ezinne Uzoka, "Why Ghana is fast becoming a hub for African Americans," *The Grio,* November 2, 2013. https://thegrio.com/2013/11/02/why-ghana-is-fast-becoming-a-hub-for-african-americans/.

2. Kathryn Schulz, "The Many Lives of Pauli Murray," *The New Yorker*, April 20, 1917, https://www.newyorker.com/magazine/2017/04/17/the-many-lives-of-pauli-murray.

3. "Julian Mayfield, Novelist and Actor Dies at 56," *The Washington Post*, October 23, 1984, https://www.washingtonpost.com/archive/local/1984/10/23/julian-mayfield-novelist-and-actor-dies-at-56/f58bb84c-ff03-48de-8cbb-c049d3d5af57/?utm_term=.9fb94eb56bd7.

4. Sandra Richards, "What is to Be Remembered?: Tourism to Ghana's Slave Castle-Dungeons," *Theatre Journal*, 57, no. 4 (2005): 622.

5. Joseph Boakye Danquah, "The Historical Significance of the Bond of 1844." *Transactions of the Historical Society of Ghana*, 3, no. 1 (1957): 6.

6. Kwame Botwe-Asamoah, *Kwame Nkrumah's Politico-Cultural Thought and Policies: An African-Centered Paradigm for the Second Phase of the African Revolution* (New York: Taylor and Francis Group, 2005), 143.

7. Richard Wright, *Black Power: Three Books from Exile* (New York: HarperCollins, 2008), 415.

8. Yakubu Saaka, "Recurrent Themes in Ghanaian Politics: Kwame Nkrumah's Legacy," *Journal of Black Studies*, 24, no. 3 (1994): 263.

9. Jennifer Hasty, "From Culture of Silence to Culture of Contest: Hegemony, Legitimacy and the Press in Ghana," *Journal of Cultural Studies*, 3, no. 2 (2001): 348–59.

10. "Member Parties," International Democratic Union, accessed May 28, 2018. https://www.idu.org/members/.

11. Delali Adogla-Bessa, "Nana Addo congratulates Trump, lauds Hillary for conceding," City 97.3 fm citionline November 9, 2016, http://citifmonline.com/2016/11/09/nana-addo-congratulates-trump-lauds-hillary-for-conceding/.

12. Janelle Wong, S. Karthick Ramakrishnan, Taeku Lee, and Jane Junn, *Asian American Political Participation: Emerging Constituents and Their Political Identities* (New York: Russell Sage Foundations), 20.

13. John Dramani Mahama, *My First Coup d'Etat: and Other True Stories from the Lost Decades of Africa* (New York: Bloomsbury, 2012), 211.

14. Thomas Hardy, "Gary Elects its First White Mayor Since 1967," *Chicago Tribune*, November 8, 1995, http://articles.chicagotribune.com/1995-11-08/news/9511090068_1_white-mayors-mayor-thomas-barnes-democrat-scott-king.

15. Ken Coleman, "Will Michigan Ever Have a Black Governor?" *Black Detroit*, February 2017, http://www.blacdetroit.com/BLAC-Detroit/February-2017/Will-Michigan-Ever-Have-a-Black-Governor/.

16. Akua Djanie, "George Bush Highway. In Ghana?" *NewAfrican*, June 20, 2012, http://newafricanmagazine.com/george-bush-highway-in-ghana/.

## Chapter 1

1. Simon Schama, *Rough Crossings: The Slaves, the British, and the American Revolution* (New York: HarperCollins Publishers, 2006), 9.

2. James T. Campbell, *Middle Passages: African American Journeys to Africa, 1787–2005* (New York: Penguin Group. 2006), 22–23.

3. A. P. Kup, *A History of Sierra Leone, 1400–1787* (Cambridge, England: Cambridge at the University Press, 1962), 1.

4. J. Lorand Matory, "The Gullah and the Black Atlantic," *Footsteps: African American History*, 3, no. 2 (2001), 10–11.

5. Ella Baker, "Back To Africa Movement." In *The Cambridge Guide to African American History* (New York: The Cambridge University Press, 2016), 25.

6. Nia Imani Cantey, et al., "Historically Black Colleges and Universities: Sustaining a Culture of Excellence in the Twenty-First Century," *Journal of African American Studies*, 17, no. 2 (2013), 143.

7. Kwame Nkrumah, *Ghana: The Autobiography of Kwame Nkrumah* (New York: International Publishers, 1957), 31.

8. Marika Sherwood, *Kwame Nkrumah: The Years Abroad* (Legon, Ghana: Freedom Publications, 1996), 61.

9. Ibid., 50–52.

10. Nkrumah, 1957, 33.

11. Sherwood, 70.

12. Nkrumah, 1957, 51.

13. Ibid., 52–55.

14. Ibid., 102.

15. Roger Gocking, *The History of Ghana* (Westport, CT: Greenwood Press, 2005), 95.
16. F. K. Buah, *A History of Ghana* (London: MacMillan Education LTD, 1998), 159–60.
17. Ibid., 161–63.
18. Campbell, 317–18.
19. Ibid., 318 and 320.
20. W. E. B. Du Bois, "The Talented Tenth," in *The Negro Problem*, ed. Booker T. Washington (New York: Arno Press, 1969), 75.
21. Obiagele Lake, "Toward a Pan-African Identity: Diaspora African Repatriates in Ghana," *Anthropological Quarterly*, 68, no. 1 (1995), 26.
22. Campbell, 335.
23. Elliott M. Rudwick, "The Niagara Movement." *The Journal of Negro History*, 40, no. 2 (1957), 17.
24. Nkrumah, 1957, 12.
25. Campbell, 334.
26. Ibid., 339.
27. Katharina Schramm, *African Homecoming: Pan-African Ideology and Contested Heritage* (Walnut Creek, CA: Left Coast Press, 2010), 65–66.
28. Ibid.
29. Campbell, 335.
30. Schramm, 66.
31. Campbell, 334.
32. Leslie Lacy, *The Rise and Fall of a Proper Negro* (New York: The McMillan Company, 1970), 175.
33. Maya Angelou, *All God's Children Need Traveling Shoes* (New York: Random House, 1986), 22–23.
34. Campbell, 341.
35. Ibid., 342.
36. Ibid., 320.
37. Angelou, 18.
38. Lacy, 156, 173–74.
39. Angelou, 22.
40. Ibid., 20.
41. Campbell, 321.
42. Ibid., 343.
43. Ibid., 324.
44. Kevin K. Gaines, *American Africans in Ghana: Black Expatriates and the Civil Rights Era* (Chapel Hill: University of North Carolina Press, 2006), 141.
45. Campbell, 331.
46. Ibid., 323.
47. Gaines, 2006, 147.
48. Lacy, 173–74.

49. David Levering Lewis, "Ghana, 1963: A Memoir," *The American Scholar*, 68, no. 1 (1989), 47.
50. Lacy, 173–74.
51. Kevin Gaines, "African-American Expatriates in Ghana: Black Radical Tradition," *Souls*, 1, no. 4 (1999), 65.
52. Ibid., 65.
53. Campbell, 336.
54. Ibid., 351.
55. Ibid., 321.
56. Lacy, 175.
57. Gaines, 2006, 143.
58. Leroy S. Hodges, Jr., *Portrait of an Expatriate: William Gardner Smith, Writer* (Westport, CT: Greenwood Press, 1985), 72.
59. Ibid., 76.
60. Ibid., 77.
61. Ibid., 79.
62. Campbell, 321.
63. David Jenkins, *Black Zion: Africa, Imagined and Real, as seen by Today's Blacks* (New York: Harcourt Brace Jovanovich, 1975), 167.
64. Lacy, 175.
65. Gaines, 1999, 68.
66. Angelou, 128.
67. Campbell, 352.
68. Ernest Dunbar, *The Black Expatriates: A Study of American Negroes in Exile* (New York: E. P. Dutton & Co., Inc, 1968), 101.
69. Angelou, pp. 128–42.
70. Ronald Walters, *Pan Africanism in the African Diaspora: An Analysis of Modern Afrocentric Political Movements* (Detroit, MI: Wayne State University Press, 1997), 118.
71. Lacy, 160.
72. Gaines, 2006, 134.
73. Lacy, 179.
74. Ibid., 170.
75. Ibid., 177.
76. Gaines, 1999, 69.
77. E Gyimah-Boadi and Richard Asante, *Ethnic Structure, Inequality and the Governance of the Public Sector in Ghana* (Geneva, Switzerland: United Nations Research Institute for Social Development, 2004), 23.
78. Ibid., 30.
79. Ibid.
80. Buah, 184.
81. Ama Biney, *The Political and Social Thought of Kwame Nkrumah* (New York: Palgrave MacMillan, 2011), 86.

82. Ibid., 125.
83. Ibid., 133.
84. John Samuel Pobee, *Religion and Politics in Ghana* (Accra, Ghana: Asempa Publishers, 1991), 31.
85. Kwesi Yankah, *Speaking for the Chief: Okyeame and the Politics of Akan Royal Oratory* (Bloomington, IN: Indiana University Press, 1995), 54.
86. Gocking, 136–37.
87. Ibid., 137.
88. Lacy, 202.
89. Angelou, 78.
90. Gaines, 1999, 68.
91. Lacy, 181–84.
92. Gaines, 2006, 115.
93. Ibid., 116–18.
94. Pauli Murray, *Song in a Weary Throat: An American Pilgrimage* (New York: Harper & Row Publishers, 1987), 342.
95. Ibid., 335.
96. Gaines, 2006, 115.
97. Godfrey Mwakikagile, *Africa 1960–1970: Chronicles and Analysis* (Dar es Salaam, Tanzania: New Africa Press, 2014), 138.
98. Lacy, 223.
99. Campbell, 345.
100. Biney, 89.
101. Ibid., 93.
102. Gocking, 148.
103. Ibid.
104. Walters, 124.
105. Campbell, 357.
106. Robert Johnson, Jr., *Why Blacks Left America for Africa: Interviews with Black Repatriates, 1971–1999* (Westport, CT: Praeger, 1999), 127.
107. Campbell, 357–61.
108. "African Countries' Names, Colonial Names, and Their Independence Days and Dates," *My Africa Now*, August 6, 2015, http://www.myafricanow.com/african-countries-independence-days-dates/.

## Chapter 2

1. Gocking, 149.
2. Ibid., 152.
3. Robert Pinkney, *Ghana Under Military Rule, 1966–1969* (London: Methuen Publishers, 1972), 43.
4. Gocking, 152.

5. Buah, 198.

6. Yaw Twumasi, "The 1969 Election," in *Politicians and Soldiers in Ghana*, ed. Dennis Austin and Robin Luckham (London: Frank Cass and Company Limited, 1975), 142.

7. Ibid.

8. Gocking, 157.

9. Buah, 200.

10. Gocking, 160.

11. Ibid., 159.

12. Laza Kekic, "The Economist Intelligence Unit's Index of Democracy," *Democracy Index*, accessed on May 29, 2018, https://www.economist.com/media/pdf/DEMOCRACY_INDEX_2007_v3.pdf.

13. Abraham H. Maslow, "A Theory of Human Motivation," *Psychological Review*, 50, no. 4 (1943), 373.

14. Gocking, 158.

15. J. D. Esseks, "Economic Policies," in *Politicians and Soldiers in Ghana, 1966-1972*, ed. Dennis Austin and Robin Luckham (London: Frank Cass, 1975), 54.

16. Ibid., 55.

17. Gocking, 161.

18. Ibid., 165.

19. Valerie Plave Bennett, "Malcontents in Uniform—the 1972 Coup d'etat," in *Politicians and Soldiers in Ghana, 1966-1972*, ed. Dennis Austin and Robin Luckham (London: Frank Cass, 1975), 305-06.

20. Gocking, 166.

21. Emmanuel Doe Ziorklui, *Ghana: Nkrumah to Rawlings . . . A Historical Sketch of Some Major Political Events in Ghana From 1957-1993* (Accra, Ghana: Em-Zed Books Centre Publishing, 1993), 326.

22. Ibid., 339.

23. Gocking, 171.

24. Ziorklui, 332.

25. Gocking, 172.

26. Safro Kwame, "Doin' Business in an African Country," *Journal of Business Ethics*, 2, no. 4 (1983), 264.

27. Gocking, 176.

28. Ibid.

29. Ibid., 177-78.

30. Ibid., 179.

31. Buah, 206.

32. Gocking, 179-80.

33. Ibid., 181.

34. Buah, 207.

35. Ibid., 208.
36. Gocking, 186.
37. Ibid., 187.
38. Ibid., 189.
39. Ibid., 190.
40. Ibid., 191.
41. Ibid., 193.
42. Gocking, 193.
43. Justin Williams, The "Rawlings Revolution" and Rediscovery of the African Diaspora in Ghana (1983-2015), *African Studies*, 74, no. 3 (2015), 369.
44. Ebenezer Obiri Addo, *Kwame Nkrumah: A Case Study of Religion and Politics in Ghana* (Lanham, MD: University Press of America, 1999), 67.
45. Gocking, 195.
46. "Ghana General Elections," *Reports of the Commonwealth Obeserver Group* (London: Commonwealth Secretariat, 2016) 3-4.
47. Ibid., 38.
48. Ibid., 50.
49. Ibid.
50. Yakubu Saaka, "Legitimizing the Illegitimate: the 1992 presidential Election as a Prelude to Ghana's Fourth Republic." In *Issues and Trends in Contemporary African Politics: Stability, Development and Democratication*, ed. George Agbango (New York: Peter Lang, 1997), 50.
51. Richard Jeffries and Clare Thomas, "The Ghanaian Elections of 1992," *African Affairs*, 92, no. 368 (1993), 331-37.
52. Ibid., 351.
53. Ibid., 352.
54. Steven Taylor, "Disputed Electoral Results in Ghana and the United States," *Journal of Global Awareness*, 5, no. 2 (2004), 58-59.
55. Nic Cheesman, *Democracy in Africa: Successes, Failures, and the Struggle for Political Reform* (Cambridge, UK: Cambridge University Press, 2015), 234-36.

## Chapter 3

1. Williams, 377.
2. Gerhard Peters and John T. Wooley, "The President's News Conference with President Jerry John Rawlings of Ghana," The American Presidency Project, last modified February 24, 1999. http://www.presidency.ucsb.edu/ws/index.php?pid=57152.
3. R. Y. Adu-Asare, "Ghana's New President Holds Pow Wow in Washington, D.C.: Urges Them to Return Home with the Know-how, Work Ethic,"

Ghana Web, July 6, 2001, https://www.ghanaweb.com/GhanaHomePage/economy/FEATURE-Ghana-s-New-President-Holds-Powwow-16414.

4. "The Joseph Project," Ministry of Tourism and Cultural Relations, last modified February 16, 2007, http://www.ghanaculture.gov.gh/modules/mod_pdf.php?archiveid=670.

5. Jake Obetsebi-Lamptey, "The Ghana Joseph Project," accessed January 19, 2018. http://www.africa-ata.org/gh9.htm.

6. "Zimbabwe Farmers Get Overtures from Ghana," Ghana Web, February 10, 2005, https://www.ghanaweb.com/GhanaHomePage/NewsArchive/Zimbabwe-farmers-get-overtures-from-Ghana-75020.

7. Williams, 381.

8. Ibid., 384.

9. Kwame Nkrumah, *Handbook of Revolutionary Warfare* (New York: International Publishers, 1968), 56.

10. "Unity of Purpose; Diversity of Action," All-African People's Revolutionary Party, last modified July 14, 2006, http://www.aaprp-intl.org/article/unity-purpose-diversity-action.

11. Nana Akufo Addo, "A Vision for Ghana and Africa," a speech given at the Heritage Foundation, Ghana Dot Com, October 21, 2015, http://www.ghanadot.com/commentary.release.npp.heritagefoundation.102115.html.

12. "International Sheroes Forum," accessed May 30, 2018, http://www.sheroesforum.com/home.cfm.

13. "Ghana loses $150m monthly due to corruption at Tema Portž—Report," *Ghana Business News*, June 14, 2013, https://www.ghanabusinessnews.com/2013/06/14/ghana-loses-150m-monthly-due-to-corruption-at-tema-port-report/.

14. "Let us cut down on corruption and loss of revenue at our ports," *News Ghana*, May 19, 2017, https://www.newsghana.com.gh/let-us-cut-down-corruption-and-loss-of-revenue-at-our-ports/.

15. Howard French, "Ghana Acts Against Broadcaster, Showing Fear of Free Media," *New York Times*, December 26, 1994, p. 07.

16. Pascal Zachary, "Tangled Roots: For African-Americans In Ghana, The Grass Isn't Always Greener," *Wall Street Journal*, March 14, 2001, p. A-1.

17. "Citizenship Act (591) of 2000," Ghana Immigration Service, accessed January 18, 2018. http://www.ghanaimmigration.org/acts%20and%20regulations/act%20591.pdf.

18. Tim Wise, "Your Whiteness is Showing," in *Who Should be First: Feminists Speak Out on the 2008 Presidential Campaign*, ed. Beverly Guy-Sheftall and Johnnetta Betsch Cole (Albany, NY: State University of New York Press, 2010), 86.

19. George M. Bob-Milliar, "Party factions and power blocs in Ghana: a case study of power politics in the National Democratic Congress." *Journal of African Studies*, 50, no. 4 (2012), 586.

20. Paul Nugent, "Living in the past: urban, rural and ethnic themes in the 1992 and 1996 elections in Ghana," *The Journal of Modern African Studies*, 37, no. 2 (1999), 287.

21. "Dumsor Borders on Ghana's Survival," Official Website of the New Patriotic Party, last modified April 19, 2015, http://newpatrioticparty.org/index.php/306-dumsor-borders-on-ghana-s-survival-nana-akufo-addo.

22. "Ghana to Eliminate English as Language of Instruction in Schools," *Amsterdam News*, March 10, 2016, http://amsterdamnews.com/news/2016/mar/10/ghana-eliminate-english-medium-instruction-schools/.

23. Nugent, 306–07.

24. "Flt.-Lt. (Rtd.) Jerry John Rawlings Profile, Ghana Web, accessed May 19, 2018. https://www.ghanaweb.com/GhanaHomePage/people/person.php?ID=166.

25. Nugent, 296.

26. Richard Jeffries, "The Ghanaian Elections of 1996: Towards the Consolidation of Democracy," *African Affairs*, vol. 97, issue 387 (April 1, 1998), 191.

27. Nugent, 297.

28. Nancy J. Weiss, *Farewell to the Party of Lincoln: Black Politics in the Age of FDR* (Princeton, NJ: Princeton University Press, 1983), 206–07.

29. David Bositis, *Blacks and the 2012 Democratic National Convention* (Washington, DC: Joint Center for Political and Economic Studies, 2012), 9.

30. "Black Demographics," http://blackdemographics.com/culture/black-politics/, accessed May 19, 2018.

31. Ibid.

32. Joseph R. Ayee,"The December 1996 General Elections in Ghana," *Electoral Studies*, 16, no. 3 (1997), 421.

33. Anthony Downs, *An Economic Theory of Democracy* (New York: Harper and Row, 1957), 118.

34. "Ghana's new capital city highway named after U.S. president George Walker Bush: Will Obama have a road in Ghana or Nigeria too?" *Otedo News Update*, June 25, 2012, http://ihuanedo.ning.com/m/group/discussion?id=2971192%3ATopic%3A76993.

35. HuiHui Wang, et al., *Ghana National Health Insurance Scheme: Improving Financial Sustainability Based on Expenditure Review* (Washington, DC: The World Bank Group, 2017), 1.

36. Lamptey.

37. "Ghana's Joseph Project Says 'Come home." National Public Radio, June 7 2007, https://www.npr.org/templates/story/story.php?storyId=10802304 (accessed January 19, 2018).

38. Harcourt Fuller, *Building the Ghanaian Nation-State: Kwame Nkrumah's Symbolic Nationalism* (New York: Palgrave McMillan, 2014), 149–50.

39. E. J. Dionne, "Did Clinton Succeed or Fail?" *The American Prospect*, December 19, 2001, http://prospect.org/article/did-clinton-succeed-or-fail.

40. Alena Samuels, "The End of Welfare as We Know it: America's Once-Robust Safety Net is No More," *The Atlantic*, April 1, 2016, https://www.theatlantic.com/business/archive/2016/04/the-end-of-welfare-as-we-know-it/476322/.

41. Emily Badger, "What happened to the millions of immigrants granted legal status under Ronald Reagan?" *The Washington Post*, November 26, 2014, https://www.washingtonpost.com/news/wonk/wp/2014/11/26/what-happened-to-the-millions-of-immigrants-granted-legal-status-under-ronald-reagan/?utm_term=.77b539fd5f28.

42. Pedro Noguera and Robert Cohen, "Remembering Reagan's Record on Civil Rights and the South African Freedom Struggle," *The Nation*, February 11, 2001, https://www.thenation.com/article/remembering-reagans-record-civil-rights-and-south-african-freedom-struggle/.

43. Ibid.

44. *Wards Cove Packing Company vs. Antonio*, 490 U.S. 642 (1989).

45. *Patterson vs. McLean Credit Union*, 491 U.S. 164 (1989).

46. *E.E.O.C. vs. Arabian American Oil Company*, 499 U.S. 244 (1991).

47. Govtrak, "HR 7152 Passage," accessed January 16, 2018. https://www.govtrack.us/congress/votes/88-1964/s409.

48. "Roll Call Vote, 101st Congress, Second Session," United States Senate, accessed January 16, 2018. https://www.senate.gov/legislative/LIS/roll_call_lists/roll_call_vote_cfm.cfm?congress=101&session=2&vote=00304#position.

49. Downs, 120.

50. Ronald Inglehart, "The Silent Revolution in Europe: Intergenerational Change in Post-Industrial Societies." *The American Political Science Review*, 64, no. 4 (1971), 991.

51. Maslow, 350–76.

52. Federal Housing Administration, *Underwriting Manual: Underwriting and Validation Procedure Under Title II of the National Housing Act* (Washington: GPO, 1938), section 980, part 3.

## Chapter 4

1. Nkrumah, 1957, 163.

2. *Ghana Investment Act*, Part II, Section 19, 1994, accessed January 4, 2018. http://images.mofcom.gov.cn/gh/accessory/201212/1354895014005.pdf).

3. Ibid., Section 18.

4. Maudlyne Ihejirika, "Brooklyn Native Gives up Everything. Now Serves Poor in Ghana." *Chicago Sun Times*, January 31, 2017, https://www.pressreader.com/usa/chicago-sun-times/20170131/281517930846605.

5. Kaylan Reid Shipanga. "African American Education on Life, Love, and Repatriation Work in Ghana," *African American in Africa*, January 30, 2017, http://www.aainafrica.com/african-american-repatriation-ghana/.

6. "Ghana: Administrative Issues for Expats," *InterNations*, accessed January 7, 2018. https://www.internations.org/ghana-expats/guide/moving-to-ghana-15777/ghana-administrative-issues-for-expats-2.

7. Ann Reed, *Pilgrimage Tourism of Diaspora Africans to Ghana* (New York: Routledge, 2015), 28.

8. "African-Americans in US and Ghana unhappy with Chieftaincy Minister's actions," MyJoyOnline.com, October 18, 2014, https://www.ghanaweb.com/GhanaHomePage/NewsArchive/African-Americans-in-US-and_Ghana-unhappy-with-Chieftaincy-Minister-s-actions-330985.

9. "ZOH TV Diasporians Living in Ghana (Earna Terefe Kassa)," a YouTube production, February 20, 2016, https://www.youtube.com/watch?v=b5KygxUEx-o.

## Chapter 5

1. "African American Association donates to two institutions," *Africultures Les Monde en Relation,* January 2018, http://africultures.com/murmures/?no=20671.

2. "We're supporting the African American Association of Ghana to bring you a series of events for #BHM2016," U.S. Embassy of Ghana, last modified February 4, 2016. https://twitter.com/usembassyghana/status/695321686523187200.

3. African American Association of Ghana, "2017 Programs," accessed May 26, 2018. http://www.aaaghana.org/events2017.php).

4. Efam Dovi, "African-Americans resettle in Ghana," *Africa Renewal Online*, April 2015, http://www.un.org/africarenewal/magazine/april-2015/african-americans-resettle-africa.

5. "The Diaspora Africa Forum," accessed May 28, 2018. http://www.ghanadiasporahs.org/gdhs-daf/.

6. "The Six Regions of the African Union," *West Africa Brief*, last modified on June 2, 2017, http://www.west-africa-brief.org/content/en/six-regions-african-union.

7. William W. Sales, Jr., *From Civil Rights to Black Liberation* (Boston: South End Press, 1994), 101–106.

8. "African Union Diaspora Africa Forum Historical Liaison with Leading Women of the African Diaspora," *The Voice, African News Magazine*, January 23, 2016, https://www.thevoicenewsmagazine.com/african-news/politics/entry/603-african-union-diaspora-african-forum-au-daf-historical-liaison-with-leading-women-of-the-african-diaspora.

9. "African Union Diaspora African Forum," *AMIP News*, October 9, 2010, https://us-africarelationsupdates.blogspot.com/2010/10/african-union-diaspora-african-forum.html.

10. Ibid.

11. Christian Lund, "'Bawku is still volatile': ethno-political con£ict and state recognition in Northern Ghana." *Journal of Modern African Studies* 41, no. 4 (2003), 589.

12. Reed, 148.

13. Godfrey Mwakikagile, *Relations Between Africans and African Americans: Misconceptions, Myths and Realities* (Dar es Salaam, Tanzania: New Africa Press, 2007), 263–64.

14. George M. Bob-Milliar, "Chieftaincy, Diaspora, and Development: The Institution of Nkɔsuohene in Ghana," *African Affairs* 108, no. 433 (2009), p. 552.

15. Reed, 148–149.

16. "My Visit to Fihankra Township," last modified June 10, 2013, https://www.youtube.com/watch?v=zXEWsmCsZeE&feature=youtu.be.

17. "Court throws out Chieftaincy Minister's case against leaders of African-American community," Myjoyonline.com, January 28, 2016, https://www.myjoyonline.com/news/2016/January-28th/court-throws-out-chieftaincy-ministers-case-against-leaders-of-african-american-community.php.

18. "Court refuses bail for the alleged African Americans' killers." *Ghana News Agency*, May 15, 2015, http://www.ghananewsagency.org/print/89483.

19. Emmanuel Ebo Hawkson, "Man, 22, to die by hanging for killing 2 African-Americans in Akwamufie," Graphic Online, November 27, 2017, https://www.graphic.com.gh/news/general-news/man-22-to-die-by-hanging-for-killing-2-african-americans-in-akwamufie.html.

20. Edem Mensah-Tsotorme, "Fihankra Killer Murdered Three More," *The Ghanaian Times*, July 30, 2015, http://www.ghanaiantimes.com.gh/fihankra-killer-murdered-3-more/.

21. Bob-Milliar, 2009, 545.

22. Ibid., 547.

23. T. C. McCaskie, "The Life and Afterlife of Yaa Asantewaa." *Africa: The Journal of the International African Institute*, 7, no. 2 (2007), 176.

24. Schramm, 241.

# Chapter 6

1. Jeffrey Blankfort, "Jews in the Media 4.3.2003," Worldpeace365, February 12, 2016, https://worldpeace365.wordpress.com/2016/02/12/jews-in-the-media-4-3-2003/.

2. Carl Russell Fish, "Carl Schurz: The American," *The Wisconsin Magazine of History*, vol. 12, no. 4 (June 1929), 345–58.

3. Willi Paul Adams, *Ethnic Leadership and the German-Born Members of the U.S. House of Representatives, 1862–1945* (Berlin, Germany: John F. Kennedy-Institut für Nordamerikastudien, 1996), 33–42.

4. Gerald W. McFarland, "The New York Mugwumps of 1884: A Profile," *Political Science Quarterly*, vol. 78, no. 1 (March 1963), 46.

5. Dara Lind, "State of the Union 2016: Why Mario Diaz-Balart is delivering the Republican Response in Spanish," *Vox*, January 12, 2016, https://www.vox.com/2016/1/12/10755710/republican-response-spanish-diaz-balart.

6. William E. Nelson, *Black Atlantic Politics: Dilemmas of Political Empowerment in Boston and Liverpool* (Albany, NY: State University of New York Press, 2000), 35.

7. William H. Flanigan and Nancy H. Zingale, "The Measurement of Electoral Change." *Political Methodology*, vol. 1, no. 3 (Summer 1974), 55.

8 Jeffrey Frank, "The Willkie What-If: F.D.R.'s Hybrid-Party Plot." *The New Yorker*, July 28, 2015, https://www.newyorker.com/news/daily-comment/the-willkie-what-if-f-d-r-s-hybrid-party-plot.

9. Anakwa Dwamena, "Ghanaians put their arms around New York." *Africa is a Country*, March 31, 2017, http://africasacountry.com/2017/03/ghanaians-put-their-arms-around-new-york/.

10. James H. Meriwether, *Proudly We Can be Africans: Black Americans and Africa, 1935–1961* (Chapel Hill: University of North Carolina Press, 2002), 289n.

11. Ebere Nwaubani, *The United States and Decolonization in West Africa, 1950–1960* (Rochester, NY: University of Rochester Press, 2001), 133.

12. John Munro, *The Anticolonial Front: The African-American Freedom Struggle and Global Decolonisation, 1945–1960* (New York: Cambridge University Press, 2017), 283.

13. Ann Brown, "African Americans Visiting, Moving to Ghana in Record Numbers," *Moguldom*, November 9, 2013, https://moguldom.com/29041/african-americans-visiting-moving-ghana-record-numbers/.

# Bibliography

Adams, Willi Paul. *Ethnic Leadership and the German-Born Members of the U.S. House of Representatives, 1862–1945*. Berlin, Germany: John F. Kennedy-Institut für Nordamerikstudien, 1996.

Addo, Ebenezer Obiri. *Kwame Nkrumah: A Case Study of Religion and Politics in Ghana*. Lanham, MD: University Press of America, 1969.

Adogla-Bessa, Delali. "Nana Addo congratulates Trump, lauds Hillary for conceding." City 97.3 fm citionline. Last modified November 9, 2016, http://citifmonline.com/2016/11/09/nana-addo-congratulates-trump-lauds-hillary-for-conceding/.

Adu-Asare, R. Y. "Ghana's New President Holds Powwow with Ghanaians in Washington, DC: Urges Them to Return Home With Their Know-how, Work Ethic." Ghana Web, last modified July 6, 2001. https://www.ghanaweb.com/GhanaHomePage/economy/FEATURE-Ghana-s-New-President-Holds-Powwow-16414.

"African American Association donates to two institutions," Africultures Les Monde en Relation, January 2018, http://africultures.com/murmures/?no=20671.

African American Association of Ghana. "2017 Programs," accessed on May 26, 2018. http://www.aaaghana.org/events2017.php.

"African-Americans in US and Ghana unhappy with Chieftaincy Minister's actions." MyJoyOnline.com, October 18, 2014. https://www.ghanaweb.com/GhanaHomePage/NewsArchive/African-Americans-in-US-and_Ghana-unhappy-with-Chieftaincy-Minister-s-actions-330985.

"African Countries' Names, Colonial Names, and Their Independence Days and Dates." *My Africa Now*, August 6, 2015. http://www.myafricanow.com/african-countries-independence-days-dates/.

"African Union Diaspora Africa Forum Historical Liaison with Leading Women of the African Diaspora." *The Voice, African News Magazine*, 17, January 23, 2016. https://www.thevoicenewsmagazine.com/african-news/politics/

entry/603-african-union-diaspora-african-forum-au-daf-historical-liaison-with-leading-women-of-the-african-diaspora.

"African Union Diaspora African Forum." *AMIP News*, October 10, 2010. https://us-africarelationsupdates.blogspot.com/2010/10/african-union-diaspora-african-forum.html.

"Akufo-Addo Congratulates president-elect Donald Trump." *Daily Guide*, November 9, 2016. http://dailyguideafrica.com/akufo-addo-congratulates-president-elect-donald-trump/. Accessed on January 18, 2018.

Akufo-Ado, Nana. "A Vision for Ghana and Africa." Ghanadot.com, October 21, 2015. http://www.ghanadot.com/commentary.release.npp.heritagefoundation.102115.html.

Angelou, Maya. *All God's Children need Traveling Shoes*. New York: Random House, 1986.

Austin, Dennis, and Robin Luckham. *Politicians and Soldiers in Ghana*. London: Frank Cass and Company Limited, 1975.

Ayee, Joseph. "The December 1996 General Elections in Ghana." *Electoral Studies*, 16, no. 3 (1997), 416–27.

Badger, Emily. "What happened to the millions of immigrants granted legal status under Ronald Reagan?" *The Washington Post*, November 26, 2014. https://www.washingtonpost.com/news/wonk/wp/2014/11/26/what-happened-to-the-millions-of-immigrants-granted-legal-status-under-ronald-reagan/?utm_term=.991f609c4ec2.

Baker, Ella. "Back to Africa Movement." *The Cambridge Guide to African American History*. New York: The Cambridge University Press, 2016.

Bennett, Valerie Plave. "Malcontents in Uniform—The 1972 Coup d'état," in *Politicians and Soldiers in Ghana*, edited by Dennis Austin and Robin Luckham. London: Frank Cass, 1975.

Biney, Ama. *The Political and Social Thought of Kwame Nkrumah*. New York: Palgrave MacMillan, 2011.

"Black Demographics." Accessed May 19, 2018. http://blackdemographics.com/culture/black-politics/.

Blankfort, Jeffrey. "Jews in the Media 4.3.2003." Worldpeace365, February 12, 2016. https://worldpeace365.wordpress.com/2016/02/12/jews-in-the-media-4-3-2003/.

Bob-Milliar, George M. "Chieftaincy, Diaspora, and Development: The Institution of Nkɔsuohene in Ghana." *African Affairs*, 108, no. 433 (2009), 541–58.

———. "Party factions and power blocs in Ghana: A case study of power Politics in the National Democratic Congress." *Journal of African Studies*, 50, no. 4 (2012), 573–601.

Bositis, David. *Blacks and the 2012 Democratic National Convention*. Washington: Joint Center for Political and Economic Studies, 2012.

Botwe-Asamoah, Kwame. *Kwame Nkrumah's Politico-Cultural Thought and Policies: An African-Centered Paradigm for the Second Phase of the African Revolution.* New York: Taylor and Francis Group, 2005.

Brown, Anne. "African Americans Visiting, Moving to Ghana in Record Numbers." *Moguldom*, November 9, 2013. https://moguldom.com/29041/african-americans-visiting-moving-ghana-record-numbers/.

Buah, F. K. *A History of Ghana.* London: MacMillan Education LTD., 1998.

Campbell, James T. *Middle Passages: African American Journeys to Africa, 1787–2005.* New York: Penguin Group, 2006.

Cantey, Nia Amini, et al. "Historically Black Colleges and Universities: Sustaining a Culture of Excellence in the Twenty-First Century. *Journal of African American Studies*, 17, no 2. (2013), 142–53.

Cheeseman, Nic. *Democracy in Africa: Successes, Failures, and the Struggle for Political Reform.* Cambridge, UK: Cambridge University Press, 2015.

"Citizenship Act (591) of 2000." Ghana Immigration Service, accessed January 18, 2008. http://www.ghanaimmigration.org/acts%20and%20regulations/act%20591.pdf.

Coleman, Ken. "Will Michigan Ever Have a Black Governor?" *Black Detroit*, February 2017. http://www.blacdetroit.com/BLAC-Detroit/February-2017/Will-Michigan-Ever-Have-a-Black-Governor/.

"Court Refuses bail for the alleged African Americans' killers." *Ghana News Agency*, May 15, 2015. http://www.ghananewsagency.org/print/89483.

"Court throws out Chieftaincy Minister's case against leaders of African-American community." Myjoyonline.com, January 28, 2016. https://www.myjoyonline.com/news/2016/January-28th/court-throws-out-chieftaincy-ministers-case-against-leaders-of-african-american-community.php.

Danquah, Joseph Boakye. "The Historical Significance of the Bond of 1844." *Transactions of the Historical Society of Ghana*, 3, no. 1 (1957), 3–29.

Diaspora Africa Forum, accessed May 28, 2018. http://www.ghanadiasporahs.org/gdhs-daf/.

Dionne, E. J. "Did Clinton Succeed or Fail?" *The American Prospect*, December 19, 2001. http://prospect.org/article/did-clinton-succeed-or-fail.

Djanie, Akua. "George Bush Highway. In Ghana?" *New African*, July 20, 2012. http://newafricanmagazine.com/george-bush-highway-in-ghana/.

Dovi, Efam. "African-Americans resettle in Ghana." *Africa Renewal Online*, April 2015. http://www.un.org/africarenewal/magazine/april-2015/african-americans-resettle-africa.

Downs, Anthony. *An Economic Theory of Democracy.* New York: Harper and Row, 1957.

Du Bois, W. E. B. "The Talented Tenth," in *The Negro Problem*, edited by Booker T. Washington. New York: Arno Press, 1969.

"Dumsor Borders on Ghana's Survival." Official website of the New Patriotic Party, last modified April 19, 2015. http://newpatrioticparty.org/index.php/306-dumsor-borders-on-ghana-s-survival-nana-akufo-addo.

Dunbar, Ernest. *The Black Expatriates: A Study of American Negroes in Exile*. New York: E. P. Dutton & Co., Inc., 1968.

Dwamena, Anakwa. "Ghanaians put their arms around New York." *Africa is a Country*, March 31, 2017. http://africasacountry.com/2017/03/ghanaians-put-their-arms-around-new-york/.

*EEOC vs. Arabian American Oil Company*, 499 U.S. 244 (1991).

Federal Housing Administration. *Underwriting Manual: Underwriting and Validation Procedure Under Title II of the National Housing Act*. Washington, DC: U.S. Government Printing Office, 1938.

Esseks, J. D. "Economic Policies," in *Politicians and Soldiers in Ghana, 1966–1972*, edited by Dennis Austin and Robin Luckam. London: Frank Cass, 1975.

Fish, Carl Russell. "Carl Schurz: The American." *The Wisconsin Magazine of History*, 12, no. 4 (1929), 345–58.

Flanigan, William H., and Nancy Zingale. "The Measurement of Electoral Change." *Political Methodology*, 1, no. 3 (1974), 49–82.

"Flt. Lt. (Rtd.) Jerry John Rawlings." Ghana Web, accessed May 19, 2018. https://www.ghanaweb.com/GhanaHomePage/people/person.php?ID=166.

Frank, Jeffrey. "The Willkie What-If: FDR's Hybrid-Party Plot." *The New Yorker*, July 28, 2015. https://www.newyorker.com/news/daily-comment/the-willkie-what-if-f-d-r-s-hybrid-party-plot.

French, Howard. "Ghana Acts Against Broadcaster, Showing Fear of Free Media," *New York Times*, December 26, 1994, p. 07.

Fuller, Harcourt. *Building the Ghanaian Nation-State: Kwame Nkrumah's Symbolic Nationalism*. New York: Palgrave McMillan, 2014.

Gaines, Kevin K. *African Americans in Ghana: Black Expatriates and the Civil Rights Era*. Chapel Hill: University of North Carolina Press, 2006.

———. "African-American Expatriates in Ghana: Black Radical Tradition," *Souls*, 1, no. 4 (1999), 64–71.

"Ghana: Administrative Issues for Expats." *InterNations*, accessed on January 7, 2018. https://www.internations.org/ghana-expats/guide/moving-to-ghana-15777/ghana-administrative-issues-for-expats-2.

"Ghana to Eliminate English as Language of Instruction in Schools," *Amsterdam News*, March 10, 2016. http://amsterdamnews.com/news/2016/mar/10/ghana-eliminate-english-medium-instruction-schools.

"Ghana Investment Act." Part II, Section, 19, 1994. Accessed January 4, 2018. http://images.mofcom.gov.cn/gh/accessory/201212/1354895014005.pdf.

"Ghana loses $150m monthly due to corruption at Tema Port—Report," *Ghana Business News*, June 14, 2013. https://www.ghanabusinessnews.com/2013/06/14/ghana-loses-150m-monthly-due-to-corruption-at-tema-port-report/.

"Ghana's new capital city highway named after U.S. President George Walker Bush: Will Obama have a road in Ghana or Nigeria too?" *Otedo News Update*, June 25, 2002. http://ihuanedo.ning.com/m/group/discussion?id=2971192%3ATopic%3A76993.

Gocking, Roger S. *The History of Ghana*. Westport, CT: Greenwood Press, 2005.

Govtrak. "HR 7152 Passage." Accessed January 16, 2018. https://www.govtrack.us/congress/votes/88-1964/s409.

Gyimah-Boadi, E., and Richard Asante. *Ethnic Structure, Inequality and the Governance of the Public Sector in Ghana*. Geneva, Switzerland: United Nations Research Institute for Social Development, 2004.

Hardy, Thomas. "Gary Elects its First White Mayor Since 1967." *Chicago Tribune*, November 8, 1995. November 8, 1995, http://articles.chicagotribune.com/1995-11-08/news/9511090068_1_white-mayors-mayor-thomas-barnes-democrat-scott-king.

Hasty, Jennifer. "Rites of Passage, Routes of Redemption: Emancipation Tourism and the Wealth of Culture." *Africa Today*, vol. 49, no. 2 (2002), 47–76.

———. "From Culture of Silence to Culture of Contest: Hegemony, Legitimacy and the Press in Ghana." *Journal of Cultural Studies*, 3, no. 2 (2001), 348–59.

Hawkson, Emmanuel Ebo. "Man, 22, to die by hanging for killing 2 African-Americans in Akwamufie." *Graphic Online*, November 24, 2017. https://www.graphic.com.gh/news/general-news/man-22-to-die-by-hanging-for-killing-2-african-americans-in-akwamufie.html.

Hodges, Jr., Leroy S. *Portrait of an Expatriate: William Gardner Smith, Writer*. Westport, CT: Greenwood Press, 1985.

Ihejirika, Maudlyne. "Brooklyn Native Gives Up Everything. Now Serves Poor in Ghana." *Chicago Sun Times*, January 31, 2017. https://www.pressreader.com/usa/chicago-sun-times/20170131/281517930846605.

"International Sheroes Forum." Accessed May 30, 2018. http://www.sheroesforum.com/home.cfm.

Jeffries, Richard. "The Ghanaian Elections of 1996." *African Affairs*, 97, no. 387 (1998), 189–208.

Jeffries, Richard, and Clare Thomas. "The Ghanaian Elections of 1992." *African Affairs*, 92, no. 368 (1993), 331–66.

Jenkins, David. *Black Zion: Africa, Imagined and Real, as seen by Today's Blacks*. New York: Harcourt Brace Jovanovich, 1975.

Johnson, Jr., Robert. *Why Blacks Left America for Africa: Interviews with Black Repatriates, 1971–1999*. Westport, CT: Praeger, 1999.

"The Joseph Project." Ministry of Tourism and Diasporan Relations. Last modified February 20, 2007. http://www.ghanaculture.gov.gh/modules/mod_pdf.php?archiveid=670.

"Julian Mayfield, Novelist and Actor Dies at 56," *The Washington Post*, October 23, 1984, https://www.washingtonpost.com/archive/local/1984/10/23/

julian-mayfield-novelist-and-actor-dies-at-56/f58bb84c-ff03-48de-8cbb-c049d3d5af57/?utm_term=.9fb94eb56bd7.

Kekic, Laza. "The Economist Intelligence Unit's Index of Democracy," *Democracy Index*, (2007), 1-10. Accessed on May 17, 2018. https://www.economist.com/media/pdf/DEMOCRACY_INDEX_2007_v3.pdf.

Kup, A. P. *A History of Sierra Leone*. Cambridge, England: Cambridge at the University Press, 1962.

Kwame, Safro. "Doin' Business in an African Country." *Journal of Business Ethics*, 2, no. 4, (1983), 263-68.

Lacy, Leslie. *The Rise and Fall of a Proper Negro*. New York: The McMillan Company, 1970.

Lake, Obiagele. "Toward a Pan-African Identity: Diaspora African Repatriates in Ghana," *Anthropological Quarterly*, 68, no. 1 (1995), 21-36.

"Let us cut down on corruption and loss of revenue at our ports," *News Ghana*, May 19, 2017. https://www.newsghana.com.gh/let-us-cut-down-corruption-and-loss-of-revenue-at-our-ports/.

Lewis, David Levering. "Ghana, 1963: A Memoir," *The American Scholar*, 68, no. 1 (1989), 39-60.

Lind, Dara. "State of the Union 2016: Why Mario Diaz-Balart is delivering the Republican response in Spanish." *Vox*, January 12, 2016. https://www.vox.com/2016/1/12/10755710/republican-response-spanish-diaz-balart.

Lund, Christian. " 'Bawku is still volatile': Ethno-political conflict and state recognition in Northern Ghana." *Journal of Modern African Studies*, 41, no 4 (2003), 587-610.

McCaskie, T. C. "The Life and Afterlife of Yaa Asantewaa." Africa: The Journal of the *International African Institute*, 7, no. 2, (2007), 151-79.

McFarland, Gerald W. "The New York Mugwumps of 1884: A Profile." *Political Science Quarterly*, 78, no. 1 (1963), 40-58

"Member Parties," International Democratic Union, accessed May 28, 2016. https://www.idu.org/members/.

Mensah-Tsotorme, Edem. "Fihankra Killer Murdered Three More." *The Ghanaian Times*, July 30, 2015. http://www.ghanaiantimes.com.gh/fihankra-killer-murdered-3-more/.

Meriwether, James H. *Proudly We Can Be Africans: Black Americans and Africa, 1935-1961*. Chapel Hill: University of North Carolina Press, 2002.

"My Visit to Fihankra Township." A YouTube production. Last modified June 10, 2013. https://www.youtube.com/watch?v=zXEWsmCsZeE&feature=youtu.be.

Mahama, John Dramani. *My First Coup d'état: And Other True Stories from the Lost Decades of Africa*. New York: Bloomsbury, 2012.

Maslow, Abraham. "A Theory of Human Motivation," *Psychological Review*, 50, no. 4 (1943), 370-96.

Matory, J. Lorand. "The Gullah and the Black Atlantic," *Footsteps: African American History*, 3, no. 2 (2001), 10–11.

Munro, John. *The Anticolonial Front: The African-American Freedom Struggle and Global Decolonisation, 1945–1960*. New York: Cambridge University Press, 2017.

Murray, Pauli. *Song in a Weary Throat: An American Pilgrimage*. New York: Harper & Row Publishers, 1987.

Mwakikagile, Godfrey. *Relations Between Africans and African Americans: Misconceptions, Myths and Realities*. Dar es Salaam, Tanzania: New African Press, 2007.

———. *Africa 1960–1970: Chronicles and Analysis*. Dar es Salaam, Tanzania: New Africa Press, 2014.

———. *The People of Ghana: Ethnic Diversity and National Unity*. Dar es Salaam, Tanzania: New Africa Press, 2017.

Nkrumah, Kwame. Ghana: The Autobiography of Kwame Nkrumah. New York: International Publishers, 1957.

———. *Handbook of Revolutionary Warfare*. New York: International Publishers, 1968.

Noguera, Pedro, and Robert Cohen. "Remembering Reagan's Record on Civil Rights and the South African Freedom Struggle." *The Nation*, February 11, 2001. https://www.thenation.com/article/remembering-reagans-record-civil-rights-and-south-african-freedom-struggle/.

Nugent, Paul. "Living in the past: urban, rural and ethnic themes in the 1992 and 1996 elections in Ghana." *The Journal of Modern African Studies*, 37, no. 2 (1999), 287–319.

Nwaubani, Ebere. *The United States and Decolonization in West Africa, 1950–1960*. Rochester, NY: University of Rochester Press, 2001.

Obetsebi-Lamptey, Jake. "The Ghana Joseph Project," Ghana Ministry of Tourism and Diasporan Relations, 2007. Accessed on January 18, 2018. http://www.africa-ata.org/gh9.htm.

*Patterson vs. McLean Credit Union*, 491 U.S. 164 (1989).

Peters, Gerhard, and John T. Wooley. "The President's News Conference with President Jerry John Rawlings of Ghana," The American Presidency Project, last modified February 24, 1999. http://www.presidency.ucsb.edu/ws/index.php?pid=57152.

Pinkney, Rogert. *Ghana Under Military Rule, 1966–1969*. London: Methuen Publishers, 1972.

Pobee, John Samuel. *Religion and Politics in Ghana*. Accra, Ghana: Asempa Publishers, 1991.

Reed, Ann. *Pilgrimage Tourism of Diaspora Africans to Ghana*. New York: Routledge, 2015.

*Reports of the Commonwealth Observer Group*. Ghana General Elections. London: Commonwealth Secretariat, 2016.

Richards, Sandra. "What is to be Remembered? Tourism to Ghana's Slave Castle-Dungeons," *Theatre Journal*, 57, no. 4 (2005), 617–37.

Rudwick, Elliott M. "The Niagara Movement." *The Journal of Negro History*, 40, no. 2 (1957), 177–200.

Saaka, Yakubu. "Recurrent Themes in Ghanaian Politics: Kwame Nkrumah's Legacy." *Journal of Black Studies*, 24, no. 3 (1994), 263–80.

Schama, Simon. *Rough Crossings: The Slaves, the British, and the American Revolution*. New York: HarperCollins Publishers, 2006.

Schramm, Katharina. *African Homecoming: Pan African Ideology and Contested Heritage*. Walnut Creek, CA: Left Coast Press, 2010.

Sales, William W. *From Civil Rights to Black Liberation*. Boston: South End Press, 1994.

Schulz, Kathryn. "The Many Lives of Pauli Murray." *The New Yorker*, April 17, 2017, https://www.newyorker.com/magazine/2017/04/17/the-many-lives-of-pauli-murray.

Sherwood, Marika. *Kwame Nkrumah: The Years Abroad*. Legon, Ghana: Freedom Publications, 1996.

Shipanga, Kaylan Reid. "African American Education on Life, Love, and Repatriation Work in Ghana." *African American in Africa*. Last modified January 30, 2017. http://www.aainafrica.com/african-american-repatriation-ghana.

Taylor, Steven. "Disputed Electoral Results in Ghana and the United States." *Journal of Global Awareness*, 5, no. 2 (2004), 54–64.

"The Six Regions of the African Union." *West Africa Brief*, last modified on June 2, 2017. http://www.west-africa-brief.org/content/en/six-regions-african-union.

Twumasi, Yaw. "The 1969 Election," in *Politicians and Soldiers in Ghana*, edited by Dennis Austin and Robin Luckham. London: Frank Cass and Company Limited, 1975.

"Roll Call Vote, 101st Congress, Second Session," United States Senate, accessed January 16, 2018. https://www.senate.gov/legislative/LIS/roll_call_lists/roll_call_vote_cfm.cfm?congress=101&session=2&vote=00304#position.

"Unity of Purpose, Diversity of Action." All African People's Revolutionary Party. Last modified July 14, 2016. http://www.aaprp-intl.org/article/unity-purpose-diversity-action.

Uzoka, Ezine. "Why Ghana is fast becoming a hub for African Americans." *The Grio*, November 2, 2013. https://thegrio.com/2013/11/02/why-ghana-is-fast-becoming-a-hub-for-african-americans/.

Walters, Ronald. *Pan Africanism in the African Diaspora: An Analysis of Modern Afrocentric Political Movements*. Detroit: Wayne State University Press, 1997.

Wang, HuiHui, et al. *Ghana National Health Insurance Scheme: Improving Financial Sustainability Based on Expenditure Review*. Washington, DC: The World Bank Group, 2017.

*Wards Cove Packing Company vs. Atonio*, 490 U.S. 642 (1989).

Weiss, Nancy J. *Farewell to the Party of Lincoln: Black Politics in the Age of FDR.* Princeton, NJ: Princeton University Press, 1983.

"We're supporting the African American Association of Ghana to bring you a series of events for #BHM2016." United States Embassy of Ghana, last modified February 4, 2016. https://twitter.com/usembassyghana/status/695321686523187200.

Williams, Justin. "The 'Rawlings Revolution' and Rediscovery of the African Diaspora in Ghana (1983-2015)." *African Studies*, 74, no. 3 (2015), 366-87.

Wise, Tim. "Your Whiteness is Showing," in *Who Should be First: Feminists Speak Out on the 2008 Presidential Campaign,* edited by Beverly Guy-Sheftall and Johnnetta Betsch Cole. Albany, NY: State University of New York Press, 2010, pp. 85–87.

Wong, Janelle, et al. *Asian American Political Participation: Emerging Constituents and Their Political Identities.* New York: Russell Sage Foundations, 2011.

Wright, Richard. *Black Power: Three Books from Exile.* New York: HarperCollins, 2008.

Yankah, Kwesi. *Speaking for the Chief: Okyeame and the Politics of Akan Royal Oratory.* Bloomington: Indiana University Press, 1995.

Zachary, Pascal. "Tangled Roots: For African-Americans in Ghana, the Grass Isn't Always Greener." *Wall Street Journal*, March 14, 2001, A-1.

"Zimbabwe Farmers Get Overtures from Ghana." Ghana Web, February 10, 2005. https://www.ghanaweb.com/GhanaHomePage/NewsArchive/Zimbabwe-farmers-get-overtures-from-Ghana-75020.

Zorklui, Emmanuel Doe. *Ghana: Nkrumah to Rawlings . . . A Historical Sketch of Some Major Political Events in Ghana from 1957-1993.* Accra, Ghana: Em-Zed Books Centre Publishing, 1993.

# Index

Abzug, Bella, 92
Acheampong, Ignatius, 26, 27, 28, 29
African American Association of Ghana (AAAG), xvi, xxi, 75–78, 76 (illustration), 98–99
*Africa* Magazine, 26
*African Review*, 11
African National Congress, 84
African Union (AU), 55–56, 80, 84–85
African Youth Improvement Foundation, 69, 70
Afrifa, Akwasi, 22, 29
Aidoo, Chekesha, 72
Aiken, George, 60
Akans, xiv, 3, 23, 24, 30, 41, 61, 86, 87
Akbar, Na'im, 89
Akoma Academy, 72
Akpan, Kwadwo Oluwale, 85–87, 88, 90, 99
Akpan, Goloi Osakwe, 87, 88
Akpan, Majewa, 87, 88
Akuffo, Fred, 28
Akuffo-Addo, Nana, xix (illustration), xxiii, 39, 47, 95, 101
Akwamu Traditional Area, 86, 87
Aliens Compliance Order, 24

All African People's Revolutionary Party (AAPRP), xxii, 38, 39, 46, 61
Allston, Carlos, 9
American Colonization Society, 2
Angelou, Maya (Maya Make), 8, 9, 10, 12, 16
Ankrah, Joseph Arthur, 18, 22
Anlo Youth Organization, 14
Armed Forces Revolutionary Council (AFRC), 21, 29, 30, 94
Asante, Molefi, 89
Ashanti tribe, 5, 7, 14, 18, 26, 36, 89, 90
Ashanti Region, 32, 47, 71
Avoidance of Discrimination Act, 15

Barnett, Claude, 5
Benin, 100
Bennett, Ereika, 80, 81, 82–85
Berlin Conference, 14
Blanchard, James, xxiii
Boahen, Adu, xviii
Boateng, Akosua, 71–72
Bob-Millar, George, xiv
Bond, Horace Mann, 5, 9
Bond, Julian, 5, 9
Bond, Max, 9
Boone, Sylvia, 9

Boyd, Mona, 37
Brandeis, Louis, 92
Brentano, Lorenz, 93
Bush, George Herbert Walker, 58, 60
Bush, George Walker, xxiii, 55
Busia, Kofi Abrefa, xvii, xix, 5, 21, 22, 23, 24, 25, 26

Campbell, James T., xii, 8, 11–12
Cabo Verde (Cape Verde), 100
Case, Clifford, 60
Central Intelligence Agency (CIA), 17
Central Region, 41
Children's Defense Fund, 40
Citizenship Act (Ghana), 47
Civil Rights Acts (of U.S. Congress), 58, 59, 60, 97
Clarke, John Henrick, 89
Clinton, Bill, 48, 56, 97
Cold War, 8, 11, 25, 31, 97
Commonwealth Observers Group, 32
Congressional Black Caucus, 82
Convention People's Party (CPP), xvii, xxi, xxiii, 4, 9, 11, 14, 17, 18, 24, 38, 50, 92, 98, 99
Cordero, Dr. Ana Livia, 9
Council on African Affairs, 8
Cross, Maddox Tristan, v
Cross III, Melvin Charles, v
Cuban Americans, 93
"Culture of Silence," xviii, 45
Cummins, Elijah, 62
Curbelo, Carlos, 93

Daanaa, Dr. Henry Seidu, 87
*Daily Graphic*, 24
Danquah, Joseph Boakye, xix, 4, 5, 7, 15–16, 63, 98
Danquah/Busia Tradition, 22, 23, 26, 28, 36
Defamation by Newspapers Decree, 27

Democratic Party (U.S.), xx, xxii, xxiii, 41, 42, 43, 44, 47, 49, 50, 52, 53, 56–60, 61, 65, 91, 95, 96, 97
Development Chiefs, xiv
Diaspora Africa Forum (DAF), xvi, 56, 75–80, 98, 99
Diaz-Balart, Mario, 93
Downs, Anthony, 54–55, 59, 63
Drake, St. Clare, 9
Dual citizenship, xviii, 35, 39, 42, 45, 47, 70
Du Bois, W. E. B.
  Death of, 8, 12
  Denied passport, 5
  *Encyclopedia Africana*, xvi, 8, 19
  Flees Cold War repression, 8, 92
  Mentor of Nkrumah, 6, 56
  Niagara Movement, 7
  Pan African Congress of 1945, 4
  Passport reinstated, 7
  Receives Ph.D. from Harvard, 7
  Visits Ghana in 1960, 7
Du Bois, Shirley Graham, xvi, 7, 8, 11, 13, 19, 93
Dudo, Cameron, 25

*Ebony* magazine, 5
Economic Community of West African States (ECOWAS), 82
*The Economist*, 25
*E.E.O.C. vs. Arabian American Oil Company*, 58
Eisenhower, Dwight David, 53
Elizabeth II, 5
"Entrepreneurials," xviii, xxii
Ewe Tribe, 23, 24, 26, 30, 31, 61

Feelings, Tom, 11
Fellowship of Reconciliation, 17
Ferguson, Missouri, 83
Fihankra, xiv, 75, 85–90

Flanigan, William, 96
Fortuyn, Pym, 31
"Forty-Eighters," 92–93
Fourth Republic
  Democratic freedom, 39
  Discouragement of refugees, 73
  Encourages foreign investment, 98
  Ministry of Tourism, 35
  Neo-liberalism of, 37
  Restrictions on foreign land ownership, 72, 86, 99
  Restrictions on small business ownership by foreigners, 68, 99
  Similarities with United States, 54
  Stability of, 100
  Term limits, 36

Ga Tribe, 23, 24
Gaines, Kevin, xii, xiv, 16
Garvin, Vicky, 11
Gary, Indiana, xxiii
Gbedmah, Koma A., 10, 22
George W. Bush Highway, xxiv, 44
Ghana Business (Promotion) Act, 24
Ghana Caribbean Association (GCA), xxi–xxii, 82
Ghana Investment Act, 68–69
Ghana National Health Insurance Scheme, 55
Ghana Television (GTV), 11
Gocking, Roger, xiii
Goldberg, Arthur, 92
Goldwater, Barry, 53, 58
Goree Island, xv
Great Britain (or U.K.), 1, 2
Great Depression, 96
Green Party, (U.S.), 48, 62

Halevi, Kohain, 73
Haley, Alex, xv
Harvard University, 7
Hasty, Jennifer, xiv

Hayes, Isaac, 89
Heritage Foundation, 39
Herve, Julian Wright, 11, 19
Howard University, 3
Hunton, Alphaeus, 8, 11, 19
Huntsman, John, 41, 43

Inglehart, Ronald, 64
International Democratic Union, xix
International Monetary Fund (IMF), 25–26, 31
Irish-Americans, 93

Jackson, Jesse, 43, 61
Jamaica, 95
Javits, Jacob, 60, 92
Jeffries, Leonard, 89
Jenkins, David, 12
Johnson, John, 5
Johnson, Lyndon Baines, 53
"Joseph Project," 36, 55, 56, 63, 69
Joyce, Brenda, 78
Junn, Jane, xx

Kalabule, 27, 28
Kaunda, Kenneth, 19
Kea, Ray, 10
Kennedy, Anthony, 57
Kennedy, John F., 12
Kilson, Martin, 9
King, Martin Luther, 5, 9, 57, 78
King, Scott, xxiii
King, Preston, 9, 10
Kɔfobiafo, 86, 99
Koch, Edward, 92
Kotoka, E. G., 22
Kufuor, John Adjekum, xxiv, 36, 37, 43, 44, 55, 56, 61–62, 82, 83

Lacy, Leslie, 8–9, 9–10, 12, 17, 18
Lee, Robert and Sarah, 9, 12
Lee, Taeku, xx

Le Pen, Jean-Marie, 31
Lewis, David Levering, xii, 9, 10
Lewis, John, 62
Liberia, 1–2
Limman, Hilla, xviii, 29
Lincoln University, 3, 15
Liverpool, England, 93
London School of Economics, 4
Long, Russell, 60
Lucas, William, xxiii
Lumumba, Patrice, 13

Mahama, John Dramani, xix, xxii–xxiii, 41, 43, 50, 69, 72
Markham, Joyce, 17
Marley, Rita, 89
Marshall, Thurgood, 58–59
Maslow, Abraham, 25, 64, 65
Mauritius, 100
Mayfield, Julian, xii, 9, 10, 12, 92
McCarthyism, 6
McCaskie, T. C., 89
McKinney, Cynthia, 47–48, 62
*Middle Passages,* xii
Mills, John Atta, 38, 44, 49, 50, 51 (illustration), 55, 63
Mills, Dr. Nkrumah, 86
Moore, E. N., 26
Moses, Bob, 19
Murray, Pauli, xii, xvi, 16–17
Muslim Action Party, 14
Mwakikagile, Godfrey, xiv

National Alliance of Liberals (NAL), 22, 23
National Association for the Advancement of Colored People (NAACP), 7
National Democratic Congress (NDC), xviii–xix, xx, xxi, xxii, xxiii, xxiv, 32, 36, 38, 39, 42, 44, 49, 50, 52, 54, 55, 56, 61, 62, 63, 64, 72, 91, 92, 94, 95, 97, 98, 99
National Development Levy, 25
National House of Chiefs, 90, 99
National Liberation Council (NLC), 18, 21, 22, 29
National Liberation Movement (NLM), 5, 14, 22, 24
National Redemption Council, 21, 26, 27
New Patriotic Party (NPP), xviii–xix, xx, xxii, xxiii, xxiv, 32, 38, 39, 41, 42, 43, 44, 45, 47, 49, 52, 53, 54, 55, 61, 63, 69, 91, 92, 95, 96, 97, 98, 99
Nimapau, Nana Oduro II, 90
Nixon, Richard, 53
Nkɔsuohemaa, 88–89, 90, 99
Nkɔsuohene, 88, 90, 99
Nkrumah, Kwame
  Becomes President, 7
  Becomes Prime Minister, xvi, 5
  Denounced by Acheampong, 26
  Deposed in a coup, xi, xii, xvii, 18, 19
  Emulated by NDC, 91
  Invitation to African Americans, xi, xv, xviii, 6, 36, 49, 53, 56, 61, 62, 67, 92, 98
  Life in exile, 19, 38
  Life in Great Britain, 4
  Life in the United States, 3, 9
  Marxism of, 7, 31
  Meets with Malcolm X, 13
  "Osagyefo," 15, 16, 22
  Pan-Africanism of, xiii, 94
  Places African Americans in government, 47
  President's Own Guard Regiment (POGR), 18
  Proclaims Marxism and Christianity, 7

Receives honorary doctorate, 15
Splits from UGCC, 14
Support of Patrice Lumumba, 13
Supported by American expatriates, 63, 92, 97–98
Terminates Professor Wendell Pierre, 16
"Nkrumahists," xxii, 22, 23, 28
Northern People's Party, 14
Northern Region, 24, 41
Nyerere, Julius, 19
Nova Scotia, 2
Nti, Nana Appiah, 87

Obama, Barack, 41, 47, 48, 56, 73, 78, 79
Obetsebi-Lamptey, Emmanuel, 15–16, 56
Obetsebi-Lamptey, Jake, 36–37, 55, 56, 69
O'Connor, Sandra Day, 57
Organization of African Unity, 82
Organization of Afro-American Unity (OAAU), 13, 81
Otumfuo Opoku Ware II (Asantehene), 88
Otu, Michael, 22
Owusu, Victor, 29

Painter, Nell Irvin, 9
Palestinian Authority, 84
Panafest, xiii, 35, 73
*Patterson vs. McClean Credit Union*, 58
People's National Convention, xviii
People's National Party, 28, 29
People's Popular Party, 22
Phi Beta Sigma Fraternity, 3, 5, 98
Pierre, Wendell Jean, 9, 16
"The Politicals," xviii, xx, xxii, 8, 12, 13, 18, 37, 72, 92
Popular Front Party (PFP), 22, 29

Powell, Colin, 62
Powell, Jr., Adam Clayton, 5
Preventive Detention Act (PDA), 15–17
Progress Party, xvi–xviii, 22, 23, 24, 25
Provisional National Defence Council (PNDC), xvii–xviii, 21, 30, 94, 95

Quartey, Nii Kweisi, 69

Ramakrishnan, S. Karthick, xx
Randolph, A. Philip, 5
Rawlings, Jerry John
  Dictatorial phase, 29–30, 62
  Embraces economic liberalism, 31, 45, 94
  First coup, xvii, 28
  Invitation to African Americans, xvii, xviii, 35, 47, 53, 61, 62, 63, 67–68, 69, 94, 98, 99
  Invitation to foreign investors, xii
  Makes transition to democracy, xxi, 33, 54
  Pan-Africanism of, xiii
  Popularity of, 29, 63
  Second coup, xi, xvii, 30, 94
Rawlings, Konadu, 40
Reagan, Ronald, 31, 56–57
Rehnquist, William, 56, 58
Republican Party (U.S.), xix, xxii, xxiii, 40, 41, 48, 50, 53, 56–60, 61, 63, 65, 96, 97
Revolutionary War (U.S.), 1
Rhodesia, 13
"Right of Abode," 39, 61, 69, 70, 71, 98
Robertson, Frank, 9
Roosevelt, Franklin Delano, 52–53, 56, 65, 96
Ros-Lehtinen, Ileana, 93

Rubio, Marco, 93
Russell, Richard, 60

Saaka, Yakubu, 33
Salomon, Edward, 93
Sanders, Bernie, 43, 62
Sao Tome and Principe, 100
Scalia, Antonin, 56
Schramm, Katharina, xiii
Schurz, Carl, 93
Scott, Hugh, 60
Second Republic, xvii, 24, 25, 26
Senegal, xv
"Sheroes Forum," 40
Shifimo Kpee Party, 14
Sierra Leone, 1–2
Simmons, Gregory (Kwadwo Oluwale Akpan), 85
Smathers, George, 60
Smith, William Gardner, 11, 19
South Africa, xviii, 31, 57
"Southern Strategy," 97
Supreme Military Council (SMC), 21, 27, 28
Sutherland, Bill, 10, 17

Talmadge, Herman, 60
Taylor, Steven, xix (illustration), 51 (illustration)
Terefe-Kassa, Earna, 74
Thatcher, Margaret, 27
Third Republic, 28, 29
Togoland Congress, 114
Toure, Sekou, 19
Trump, Donald, xix, xxiii

UNIGOV, 27–28
United Gold Coast Convention (UGCC), 4, 14

United Party, 15, 22
University of Pennsylvania, 3

Vietnam War, 21
Volta Region, 23, 32, 33

Walters, Ronald, 18
*Ward's Cove Packing Company vs. Atonio*, 58
War Resisters League, 17
Warren, Elizabeth, 62
Weld, William, 62
West African Students Union, 4
West African National Congress, 4
Western Region, 23
Wilberforce University, 3
Wilkins, Patricia, 71, 72
Williams, Anthony, 89
Williams, Justin, xiii, 37
Williams, Marion, xxiii
Williams, Robert, 10
Willkie, Wendell, 96–97
Winneba Ideological Institute, 50
Wonder, Stevie, 89
Wong, Janelle, et al., xx
World Bank, 31
Wreeko-Brobby, Charles, 45
Wright, Jeremiah, 89
Wright, Richard, xii, xvi, 5, 11

X, Malcolm, 12–13, 81, 82

Yarbrough, Ralph, 60
Young Pioneers, 15
Youth Institute of Science and Technology, 71

Zingale, Nancy, 96
Ziorklui, Emmanuel Doe, xiii

www.ingramcontent.com/pod-product-compliance
Lightning Source LLC
Chambersburg PA
CBHW021144230426
43667CB00005B/254